MENTAL ILLNESSES AND TREATMENTS SERIES

MENTAL ILLNESSES: DESCRIPTIONS, CAUSES AND TREATMENTS

MENTAL ILLNESSES AND TREATMENTS SERIES

Mental Illnesses: Descriptions, Causes and Treatments
Jeremias Koch (Editor)
2010. ISBN:978-1-60741-652-4

MENTAL ILLNESSES AND TREATMENTS SERIES

MENTAL ILLNESSES: DESCRIPTIONS, CAUSES AND TREATMENTS

JEREMIAS KOCH
EDITOR

Nova Science Publishers, Inc.
New York

LIBRARY OF CONGRESS CATALOGING-IN-PUBLICATION DATA

Mental illnesses : descriptions, causes, and treatments / [edited by] Jeremias Koch.
 p. ; cm.
Includes bibliographical references and index.
ISBN 978-1-60741-652-4 (softcover)
1. Manic-depressive illness. 2. Dual diagnosis. I. Koch, Jeremias.
[DNLM: 1. Mental Disorders--diagnosis. 2. Mental Disorders--etiology. 3. Mental Disorders--therapy. WM 140 M5499 2009]
RC516.M47 2009
616.89'5--dc22

2009031812

Published by Nova Science Publishers, Inc. ✛ New York

CONTENTS

PREFACE

This book contains research related to mental illnesses, particularly bipolar disorder and schizophrenia. This includes information on symptoms, how the diseases develop, current treatments available, support for family members, and new directions in research. There is also a section on comorbidity as it relates to addiction and other mental illnesses.

This book consists of public domain documents which have been located, gathered, combined, reformatted, and enhanced with a subject index, selectively edited and bound to provide easy access.

Chapter 1 - Bipolar disorder, also known as manic-depressive illness, is a brain disorder that causes unusual shifts in a person's mood, energy, and ability to function. Different from the normal ups and downs that everyone goes through, the symptoms of bipolar disorder are severe. They can result in damaged relationships, poor job or school performance, and even suicide. But there is good news: bipolar disorder can be treated, and people with this illness can lead full and productive lives.

Chapter 2 - Are you feeling really "down" sometimes and really "up" other times? Are these mood changes causing problems at work, school, or home? If yes, you may have bipolar disorder, also called manic-depressive illness.

Chapter 3 - Comorbidity is a topic that our stakeholders—patients, family members, health care professionals, and others—frequently ask about. It is also a topic about which we have insufficient information, and so it remains a research priority for NIDA. This Research Report provides information on the state of the science in this area. And although a variety of diseases commonly co-occur with drug abuse and addiction (e.g. HIV, hepatitis C, cancer, cardiovascular disease), this report focuses only on the comorbidity of drug use disorders and other mental illnesses.

Chapter 4 - Schizophrenia is a chronic, severe, and disabling brain disorder that has been recognized throughout recorded history. It affects about 1 percent of Americans.

People with schizophrenia may hear voices other people don't hear or they may believe that others are reading their minds, controlling their thoughts, or plotting to harm them. These experiences are terrifying and can cause fearfulness, withdrawal, or extreme agitation. People with schizophrenia may not make sense when they talk, may sit for hours without moving or talking much, or may seem perfectly fine until they talk about what they are really thinking. Because many people with schizophrenia have difficulty holding a job or caring for themselves, the burden on their families and society is significant as well.

Available treatments can relieve many of the disorder's symptoms, but most people who have schizophrenia must cope with some residual symptoms as long as they live. Nevertheless, this is a time of hope for people with schizophrenia and their families. Many people with the disorder now lead rewarding and meaningful lives in their communities. Researchers are developing more effective medications and using new research tools to understand the causes of schizophrenia and to find ways to prevent and treat it.

In: Mental Illness   ISBN: 978-1-60741-652-4
Editor: Jeremias Koch   © 2010 Nova Science Publishers, Inc.

Chapter 1

BIPOLAR DISORDER WITH ADDENDUM BIPOLAR

National Institute of Mental Health

Bipolar disorder, also known as manic-depressive illness, is a brain disorder that causes unusual shifts in a person's mood, energy, and ability to function. Different from the normal ups and downs that everyone goes through, the symptoms of bipolar disorder are severe. They can result in damaged relationships, poor job or school performance, and even suicide. But there is good news: bipolar disorder can be treated, and people with this illness can lead full and productive lives.

More than 2 million American adults,[1] or about 1 percent of the population age 18 and older in any given year,[2] have bipolar disorder. Bipolar disorder typically develops in late adolescence or early adulthood. However, some people have their first symptoms during childhood, and some develop them late in life. It is often not recognized as an illness, and people may suffer for years before it is properly diagnosed and treated. Like diabetes or heart disease, bipolar disorder is a long-term illness that must be carefully managed throughout a person's life.

"Manic-depression distorts moods and thoughts, incites dreadful behaviors, destroys the basis of rational thought, and too often erodes the desire and will to live. It is an illness that is biological in its origins, yet one that feels psychological in the experience of it; an illness that is

unique in conferring advantage and pleasure, yet one that brings in its wake almost unendurable suffering and, not infrequently, suicide.
"I am fortunate that I have not died from my illness, fortunate in having received the best medical care available, and fortunate in having the friends, colleagues, and family that I do."

Kay Redfield Jamison, Ph.D., *An Unquiet Mind*, 1995, p. 6. (Reprinted with permission from Alfred A. Knopf, a division of Random House, Inc.)

WHAT ARE THE SYMPTOMS OF BIPOLAR DISORDER?

Bipolar disorder causes dramatic mood swings—from overly "high" and/or irritable to sad and hopeless, and then back again, often with periods of normal mood in between. Severe changes in energy and behavior go along with these changes in mood. The periods of highs and lows are called **episodes** of mania and depression.

Signs and symptoms of *mania* (or a *manic episode*) include:

- Increased energy, activity, and restlessness
- Excessively "high," overly good, euphoric mood
- Extreme irritability
- Racing thoughts and talking very fast, jumping from one idea to another
- Distractibility, can't concentrate well
- Little sleep needed
- Unrealistic beliefs in one's abilities and powers
- Poor judgment
- Spending sprees
- A lasting period of behavior that is different from usual
- Increased sexual drive
- Abuse of drugs, particularly cocaine, alcohol, and sleeping medications
- Provocative, intrusive, or aggressive behavior
- Denial that anything is wrong

A manic episode is diagnosed if elevated mood occurs with 3 or more of the other symptoms most of the day, nearly every day, for 1 week or longer. If the mood is irritable, 4 additional symptoms must be present.

Signs and symptoms of *depression* (or a *depressive episode*) include:

- Lasting sad, anxious, or empty mood
- Feelings of hopelessness or pessimism
- Feelings of guilt, worthlessness, or helplessness
- Loss of interest or pleasure in activities once enjoyed, including sex
- Decreased energy, a feeling of fatigue or of being "slowed down"
- Difficulty concentrating, remembering, making decisions
- Restlessness or irritability
- Sleeping too much, or can't sleep
- Change in appetite and/or unintended weight loss or gain
- Chronic pain or other persistent bodily symptoms that are not caused by physical illness or injury
- Thoughts of death or suicide, or suicide attempts

A depressive episode is diagnosed if 5 or more of these symptoms last most of the day, nearly every day, for a period of 2 weeks or longer.

A mild to moderate level of mania is called **hypomania.** Hypomania may feel good to the person who experiences it and may even be associated with good functioning and enhanced productivity. Thus even when family and friends learn to recognize the mood swings as possible bipolar disorder, the person may deny that anything is wrong. Without proper treatment, however, hypomania can become severe mania in some people or can switch into depression.

Sometimes, severe episodes of mania or depression include symptoms of **psychosis** (or psychotic symptoms). Common psychotic symptoms are hallucinations (hearing, seeing, or otherwise sensing the presence of things not actually there) and delusions (false, strongly held beliefs not influenced by logical reasoning or explained by a person's usual cultural concepts). Psychotic symptoms in bipolar disorder tend to reflect the extreme mood state at the time. For example, delusions of grandiosity, such as believing one is the President or has special powers or wealth, may occur during mania; delusions of guilt or worthlessness, such as believing that one is ruined and penniless or has committed some terrible crime, may appear during depression. People with bipolar disorder who have these symptoms are sometimes incorrectly diagnosed as having schizophrenia, another severe mental illness.

It may be helpful to think of the various mood states in bipolar disorder as a spectrum or continuous range. At one end is severe depression, above which is moderate depression and then mild low mood, which many people call "the blues" when it is shortlived but is termed "dysthymia" when it is chronic. Then there is normal or balanced mood, above which comes hypomania (mild to moderate mania), and then severe mania.

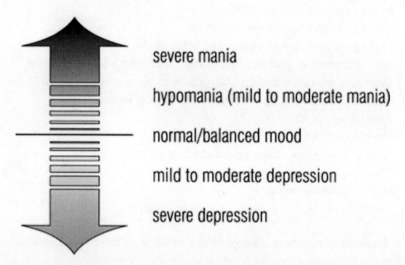

severe mania

hypomania (mild to moderate mania)

normal/balanced mood

mild to moderate depression

severe depression

In some people, however, symptoms of mania and depression may occur together in what is called a **mixed** bipolar state. Symptoms of a mixed state often include agitation, trouble sleeping, significant change in appetite, psychosis, and suicidal thinking. A person may have a very sad, hopeless mood while at the same time feeling extremely energized.

Bipolar disorder may appear to be a problem other than mental illness—for instance, alcohol or drug abuse, poor school or work performance, or strained interpersonal relationships. Such problems in fact may be signs of an underlying mood disorder.

DIAGNOSIS OF BIPOLAR DISORDER

Like other mental illnesses, bipolar disorder cannot yet be identified physiologically—for example, through a blood test or a brain scan. Therefore, a diagnosis of bipolar disorder is made on the basis of symptoms, course of illness, and, when available, family history. The diagnostic criteria for bipolar disorder are described in the *Diagnostic and Statistical Manual for Mental Disorders, fourth edition (DSM-IV).*[3]

Descriptions offered by people with bipolar disorder give valuable insights into the various mood states associated with the illness:

Depression : *I doubt completely my ability to do anything well. It seems as though my mind has slowed down and burned out to the point of being virtually useless.... [I am] haunt[ed]... with the total, the desperate hopelessness of it all.... Others say, "It's only temporary, it will pass, you will get over it," but of course they haven't any idea of how I feel, although they are certain they do. If I can't feel, move, think or care, then what on earth is the point?*

Hypomania: *At first when I'm high, it's tremendous... ideas are fast... like shooting stars you follow until brighter ones appear.... All shyness disappears, the right words and gestures are suddenly there... uninteresting people, things become intensely interesting. Sensuality is pervasive, the desire to seduce and be seduced is irresistible. Your marrow is infused with unbelievable feelings of ease, power, well-being, omnipotence, euphoria... you can do anything... but, somewhere this changes.*

Mania: *The fast ideas become too fast and there are far too many... overwhelming confusion replaces clarity... you stop keeping up with it... memory goes. Infectious humor ceases to amuse. Your friends become frightened...everything is now against the grain... you are irritable, angry, frightened, uncontrollable, and trapped.*

SUICIDE

Some people with bipolar disorder become suicidal. **Anyone who is thinking about committing suicide needs immediate attention, preferably from a mental health professional or a physician. Anyone who talks about suicide should be taken seriously.** Risk for suicide appears to be higher earlier in the course of the illness. Therefore, recognizing bipolar disorder early and learning how best to manage it may decrease the risk of death by suicide.

Signs and symptoms that may accompany suicidal feelings include:

- talking about feeling suicidal or wanting to die
- feeling hopeless, that nothing will ever change or get better

- feeling helpless, that nothing one does makes any difference
- feeling like a burden to family and friends
- abusing alcohol or drugs
- putting affairs in order (e.g., organizing finances or giving away possessions to prepare for one's death)
- writing a suicide note
- putting oneself in harm's way, or in situations where there is a danger of being killed

---

IF YOU ARE FEELING SUICIDAL OR KNOW SOMEONE WHO IS:

- call a doctor, emergency room, or 911 right away to get immediate help
- make sure you, or the suicidal person, are not left alone
- make sure that access is prevented to large amounts of medication, weapons, or
- other items that could be used for self-harm

While some suicide attempts are carefully planned over time, others are impulsive acts that have not been well thought out; thus, the final point in the box above may be a valuable *long-term* strategy for people with bipolar disorder. Either way, it is important to understand that suicidal feelings and actions are symptoms of an illness that can be treated. With proper treatment, suicidal feelings can be overcome.

WHAT IS THE COURSE OF BIPOLAR DISORDER?

Episodes of mania and depression typically recur across the life span. Between episodes, most people with bipolar disorder are free of symptoms, but as many as one-third of people have some residual symptoms. A small percentage of people experience chronic unremitting symptoms despite treatment.[4]

The classic form of the illness, which involves recurrent episodes of mania and depression, is called **bipolar I disorder.** Some people, however, never develop severe mania but instead experience milder episodes of hypomania that alternate with depression; this form of the illness is called **bipolar II disorder.** When 4 or more episodes of illness occur within a 12-month period, a person is said to have **rapid-cycling** bipolar disorder. Some people experience multiple episodes within a single week, or even within a single day. Rapid cycling tends to develop later in the course of illness and is more common among women than among men.

People with bipolar disorder can lead healthy and productive lives when the illness is effectively treated (see below— "How Is Bipolar Disorder Treated?"). Without treatment, however, the natural course of bipolar disorder tends to worsen. Over time a person may suffer more frequent (more rapid-cycling) and more severe manic and depressive episodes than those experienced when the illness first appeared.[5] But in most cases, proper treatment can help reduce the frequency and severity of episodes and can help people with bipolar disorder maintain good quality of life.

CAN CHILDREN AND ADOLESCENTS HAVE BIPOLAR DISORDER?

Both children and adolescents can develop bipolar disorder. It is more likely to affect the children of parents who have the illness.

Unlike many adults with bipolar disorder, whose episodes tend to be more clearly defined, children and young adolescents with the illness often experience very fast mood swings between depression and mania many times within a day.[6] Children with mania are more likely to be irritable and prone to destructive tantrums than to be overly happy and elated. Mixed symptoms also are common in youths with bipolar disorder. Older adolescents who develop the illness may have more classic, adult-type episodes and symptoms.

Bipolar disorder in children and adolescents can be hard to tell apart from other problems that may occur in these age groups. For example, while irritability and aggressiveness can indicate bipolar disorder, they also can be symptoms of attention deficit hyperactivity disorder, conduct disorder, oppositional defiant disorder, or other types of mental disorders more common among adults such as major depression or schizophrenia. Drug abuse also may lead to such symptoms.

For any illness, however, effective treatment depends on appropriate diagnosis. Children or adolescents with emotional and behavioral symptoms should be carefully evaluated by a mental health professional. **Any child or adolescent who has suicidal feelings, talks about suicide, or attempts suicide should be taken seriously and should receive immediate help from a mental health specialist.**

WHAT CAUSES BIPOLAR DISORDER?

Scientists are learning about the possible causes of bipolar disorder through several kinds of studies. Most scientists now agree that there is no single cause for bipolar disorder—rather, many factors act together to produce the illness.

Because bipolar disorder tends to run in families, researchers have been searching for specific genes—the microscopic "building blocks" of DNA inside all cells that influence how the body and mind work and grow—passed down through generations that may increase a person's chance of developing the illness. But genes are not the whole story. Studies of identical twins, who share all the same genes, indicate that both genes and other factors play a role in bipolar disorder. If bipolar disorder were caused entirely by genes, then the identical twin of someone with the illness would *always* develop the illness, and research has shown that this is not the case. But if one twin has bipolar disorder, the other twin is more likely to develop the illness than is another sibling.[7]

In addition, findings from gene research suggest that bipolar disorder, like other mental illnesses, does not occur because of a single gene.[8] It appears likely that many different genes act together, and in combination with other factors of the person or the person's environment, to cause bipolar disorder. Finding these genes, each of which contributes only a small amount toward the vulnerability to bipolar disorder, has been extremely difficult. But scientists expect that the advanced research tools now being used will lead to these discoveries and to new and better treatments for bipolar disorder.

Brain-imaging studies are helping scientists learn what goes wrong in the brain to produce bipolar disorder and other mental illnesses.[9,10] New brain-imaging techniques allow researchers to take pictures of the living brain at work, to examine its structure and activity, without the need for surgery or other invasive procedures. These techniques include magnetic resonance imaging (MRI), positron emission tomography (PET), and functional magnetic resonance imaging (fMRI). There is evidence from imaging studies that the brains of people with bipolar disorder may differ from the brains of healthy individuals. As the differences are more clearly identified and defined through research, scientists will gain a better understanding of the underlying causes of the illness, and eventually may be able to predict which types of treatment will work most effectively.

HOW IS BIPOLAR DISORDER TREATED?

Most people with bipolar disorder—even those with the most severe forms—can achieve substantial stabilization of their mood swings and related symptoms with proper treatment.[11,12,13] Because bipolar disorder is a recurrent illness, long-term preventive treatment is strongly recommended and almost always indicated. A strategy that combines medication and psychosocial treatment is optimal for managing the disorder over time.

In most cases, bipolar disorder is much better controlled if treatment is continuous than if it is on and off. But even when there are no breaks in treatment, mood changes can occur and should be reported immediately to your doctor. The doctor may be able to prevent a full-blown episode by making adjustments to the treatment plan. Working closely with the doctor and communicating openly about treatment concerns and options can make a difference in treatment effectiveness.

In addition, keeping a chart of daily mood symptoms, treatments, sleep patterns, and life events may help people with bipolar disorder and their families to better understand the illness. This chart also can help the doctor track and treat the illness most effectively.

Medications

Medications for bipolar disorder are prescribed by psychiatrists—medical doctors (M.D.) with expertise in the diagnosis and treatment of mental disorders. While primary care physicians who do not specialize in psychiatry also may prescribe these medications, it is recommended that people with bipolar disorder see a psychiatrist for treatment.

Medications known as "mood stabilizers" usually are prescribed to help control bipolar disorder.[11] Several different types of mood stabilizers are available. In general, people with bipolar disorder continue treatment with mood stabilizers for extended periods of time (years). Other medications are added when necessary, typically for shorter periods, to treat episodes of mania or depression that break through despite the mood stabilizer.

- Lithium, the first mood-stabilizing medication approved by the U.S. Food and Drug Administration (FDA) for treatment of mania, is often very effective in controlling mania and preventing the recurrence of both manic and depressive episodes.

- Anticonvulsant medications, such as valproate (Depakote®) or carbamazepine (Tegretol®), also can have mood-stabilizing effects and may be especially useful for difficult-to-treat bipolar episodes. Valproate was FDA-approved in 1995 for treatment of mania.
- Newer anticonvulsant medications, including lamotrigine (Lamictal®), gabapentin (Neurontin®), and topiramate (Topamax®), are being studied to determine how well they work in stabilizing mood cycles.
- Anticonvulsant medications may be combined with lithium, or with each other, for maximum effect.
- Children and adolescents with bipolar disorder generally are treated with lithium, but valproate and carbamazepine also are used. Researchers are evaluating the safety and efficacy of these and other psychotropic medications in children and adolescents. *There is some evidence that valproate may lead to adverse hormone changes in teenage girls and polycystic ovary syndrome in women who began taking the medication before age 20.*[14] *Therefore, young female patients taking valproate should be monitored carefully by a physician.*
- Women with bipolar disorder who wish to conceive, or who become pregnant, face special challenges due to the possible harmful effects of existing mood stabilizing medications on the developing fetus and the nursing infant.[15] Therefore, the benefits and risks of all available treatment options should be discussed with a clinician skilled in this area. New treatments with reduced risks during pregnancy and lactation are under study.

TREATMENT OF BIPOLAR DEPRESSION

Research has shown that people with bipolar disorder are at risk of switching into mania or hypomania, or of developing rapid cycling, during treatment with antidepressant medication.[16] Therefore, *"mood-stabilizing" medications generally are required, alone or in combination with antidepressants, to protect people with bipolar disorder from this switch.* Lithium and valproate are the most commonly used mood-stabilizing drugs today. However, research studies continue to evaluate the potential mood-stabilizing effects of newer medications.

- Atypical antipsychotic medications, including clozapine (Clozaril®), olanzapine (Zyprexa®), risperidone (Risperdal®), and ziprasidone (Zeldox®), are being studied as possible treatments for bipolar disorder. Evidence suggests clozapine may be helpful as a mood stabilizer for people who do not respond to lithium or anticonvulsants.[17] Other research has supported the efficacy of olanzapine for acute mania, an indication that has recently received FDA approval.[18] Olanzapine may also help relieve psychotic depression.[19]

- If insomnia is a problem, a high-potency benzodiazepine medication such as clonazepam (Klonopin®) or lorazepam (Ativan®) may be helpful to promote better sleep. However, since these medications may be habit-forming, they are best prescribed on a short-term basis. Other types of sedative medications, such as zolpidem (Ambien®), are sometimes used instead.

- Changes to the treatment plan may be needed at various times during the course of bipolar disorder to manage the illness most effectively. A psychiatrist should guide any changes in type or dose of medication.

- Be sure to tell the psychiatrist about all other prescription drugs, over-the-counter medications, or natural supplements you may be taking. This is important because certain medications and supplements taken together may cause adverse reactions.

- To reduce the chance of relapse or of developing a new episode, it is important to stick to the treatment plan. Talk to your doctor if you have any concerns about the medications.

THYROID FUNCTION

People with bipolar disorder often have abnormal thyroid gland function.[5] Because too much or too little thyroid hormone alone can lead to mood and energy changes, it is important that thyroid levels are carefully monitored by a physician.

People with rapid cycling tend to have co-occurring thyroid problems and may need to take thyroid pills in addition to their medications for bipolar disorder. Also, lithium treatment may cause low thyroid levels in some people, resulting in the need for thyroid supplementation.

MEDICATION SIDE EFFECTS

Before starting a new medication for bipolar disorder, always talk with your psychiatrist and/or pharmacist about possible side effects. Depending on the medication, side effects may include weight gain, nausea, tremor, reduced sexual drive or performance, anxiety, hair loss, movement problems, or dry mouth. Be sure to tell the doctor about all side effects you notice during treatment. He or she may be able to change the dose or offer a different medication to relieve them. Your medication should not be changed or stopped without the psychiatrist's guidance.

Psychosocial Treatments

As an addition to medication, psychosocial treatments—including certain forms of psychotherapy (or "talk" therapy)—are helpful in providing support, education, and guidance to people with bipolar disorder and their families. Studies have shown that psychosocial interventions can lead to increased mood stability, fewer hospitalizations, and improved functioning in several areas.[13] A licensed psychologist, social worker, or counselor typically provides these therapies and often works together with the psychiatrist to monitor a patient's progress. The number, frequency, and type of sessions should be based on the treatment needs of each person.

Psychosocial interventions commonly used for bipolar disorder are cognitive behavioral therapy, psychoeducation, family therapy, and a newer technique, interpersonal and social rhythm therapy. NIMH researchers are studying how these interventions compare to one another when added to medication treatment for bipolar disorder.

- Cognitive behavioral therapy helps people with bipolar disorder learn to change inappropriate or negative thought patterns and behaviors associated with the illness.
- Psychoeducation involves teaching people with bipolar disorder about the illness and its treatment, and how to recognize signs of relapse so that early intervention can be sought before a full-blown illness episode occurs. Psycho-education also may be helpful for family members.
- Family therapy uses strategies to reduce the level of distress within the family that may either contribute to or result from the ill person's symptoms.
- Interpersonal and social rhythm therapy helps people with bipolar disorder both to improve interpersonal relationships and to regularize their daily routines. Regular daily routines and sleep schedules may help protect against manic episodes.
- As with medication, it is important to follow the treatment plan for any psychosocial intervention to achieve the greatest benefit.

Other Treatments

- In situations where medication, psychosocial treatment, and the combination of these interventions prove ineffective, or work too slowly to relieve severe symptoms such as psychosis or suicidality, electroconvulsive therapy (ECT) may be considered. ECT may also be considered to treat acute episodes when medical conditions, including pregnancy, make the use of medications too risky. ECT is a highly effective treatment for severe depressive, manic, and/or mixed episodes. The possibility of long-lasting memory problems, although a concern in the past, has been significantly reduced with modern ECT techniques. However, the potential benefits and risks of ECT, and of available alternative interventions, should be carefully reviewed and discussed with individuals considering this treatment and, where appropriate, with family or friends.[20]
- Herbal or natural supplements, such as St. John's wort *(Hypericum perforatum)*, have not been well studied, and little is known about their effects on bipolar disorder. Because the FDA does not regulate their production, different brands of these supplements can contain different amounts of active ingredient. **Before trying herbal or natural**

supplements, it is important to discuss them with your doctor. There is
evidence that St. John's wort can reduce the effectiveness of certain
medications (see http://www.nimh.nih.gov/events/stjohnwort.cfm).[21] In
addition, like prescription antidepressants, St. John's wort may cause a
switch into mania in some individuals with bipolar disorder, especially if
no mood stabilizer is being taken.[22]

- Omega-3 fatty acids found in fish oil are being studied to determine their
  usefulness, alone and when added to conventional medications, for long-
  term treatment of bipolar disorder.[23]

A LONG-TERM ILLNESS THAT CAN BE EFFECTIVELY TREATED

Even though episodes of mania and depression naturally come and go, it is
important to understand that bipolar disorder is a long-term illness that
currently has no cure. Staying on treatment, even during well times, can help
keep the disease under control and reduce the chance of having recurrent,
worsening episodes.

DO OTHER ILLNESSES CO-OCCUR WITH BIPOLAR DISORDER?

Alcohol and drug abuse are very common among people with bipolar
disorder. Research findings suggest that many factors may contribute to these
substance abuse problems, including self-medication of symptoms, mood
symptoms either brought on or perpetuated by substance abuse, and risk factors
that may influence the occurrence of both bipolar disorder and substance use
disorders.[24] Treatment for co-occurring substance abuse, when present, is an
important part of the overall treatment plan.

Anxiety disorders, such as post-traumatic stress disorder and obsessive-
compulsive disorder, also may be common in people with bipolar disorder.[25,26]
Co-occurring anxiety disorders may respond to the treatments used for bipolar
disorder, or they may require separate treatment. For more information on anxiety
disorders, contact NIMH (see below).

HOW CAN INDIVIDUALS AND FAMILIES GET HELP
FOR BIPOLAR DISORDER?

Anyone with bipolar disorder should be under the care of a psychiatrist skilled in the diagnosis and treatment of this disease. Other mental health professionals, such as psychologists, psychiatric social workers, and psychiatric nurses, can assist in providing the person and family with additional approaches to treatment.

Help can be found at:

- University—or medical school—affiliated programs
- Hospital departments of psychiatry
- Private psychiatric offices and clinics
- Health maintenance organizations (HMOs)
- Offices of family physicians, internists, and pediatricians
-

Public community mental health centers

- People with bipolar disorder may need help to get help.
- Often people with bipolar disorder do not realize how impaired they are, or they blame their problems on some cause other than mental illness.
- A person with bipolar disorder may need strong encouragement from family and friends to seek treatment.
- Family physicians can play an important role in providing referral to a mental health professional.
- Sometimes a family member or friend may need to take the person with bipolar disorder for proper mental health evaluation and treatment.
- A person who is in the midst of a severe episode may need to be hospitalized for his or her own protection and for much-needed treatment. There may be times when the person must be hospitalized against his or her wishes.
- Ongoing encouragement and support are needed after a person obtains treatment, because it may take a while to find the best treatment plan for each individual.
- In some cases, individuals with bipolar disorder may agree, when the disorder is under good control, to a preferred course of action in the event of a future manic or depressive relapse.

- Like other serious illnesses, bipolar disorder is also hard on spouses, family members, friends, and employers.
- Family members of someone with bipolar disorder often have to cope with the person's serious behavioral problems, such as wild spending sprees during mania or extreme withdrawal from others during depression, and the lasting consequences of these behaviors.
- Many people with bipolar disorder benefit from joining support groups such as those sponsored by the National Depressive and Manic Depressive Association (NDMDA), the National Alliance for the Mentally Ill (NAMI), and the National Mental Health Association (NMHA). Families and friends can also benefit from support groups offered by these organizations. For contact information, see the "For More Information" section at the back of this booklet.

WHAT ABOUT CLINICAL STUDIES FOR BIPOLAR DISORDER?

Some people with bipolar disorder receive medication and/or psychosocial therapy by volunteering to participate in clinical studies (clinical trials). Clinical studies involve the scientific investigation of illness and treatment of illness in humans. Clinical studies in mental health can yield information about the efficacy of a medication or a combination of treatments, the usefulness of a behavioral intervention or type of psychotherapy, the reliability of a diagnostic procedure, or the success of a prevention method. Clinical studies also guide scientists in learning how illness develops, progresses, lessens, and affects both mind and body. Millions of Americans diagnosed with mental illness lead healthy, productive lives because of information discovered through clinical studies. These studies are not always right for everyone, however. It is important for each individual to consider carefully the possible risks and benefits of a clinical study before making a decision to participate.

In recent years, NIMH has introduced a new generation of "real-world" clinical studies. They are called "real-world" studies for several reasons. Unlike traditional clinical trials, they offer multiple different treatments and treatment combinations. In addition, they aim to include large numbers of people with mental disorders living in communities throughout the U.S. and receiving treatment across a wide variety of settings. Individuals with more than one mental disorder, as well as those with co-occurring physical illnesses, are encouraged to consider participating in these new studies. The main goal of the real-world studies is to improve treatment strategies and outcomes for all people with these disorders. In addition to measuring improvement in illness symptoms,the studies will evaluate how treatments influence other important, real-world issues such as quality of life, ability to work, and social functioning. They also will assess the cost-effectiveness of different treatments and factors that affect how well people stay on their treatment plans.

The Systematic Treatment Enhancement Program for Bipolar Disorder (STEP-BD) is seeking participants for the largest-ever, "realworld" study of treatments for bipolar disorder. To learn more about STEP-BD or other clinical studies, see the Clinical Trials page on the NIMH Web site http://www.nimh.nih.gov, visit the National Library of Medicine's clinical trials database http://www.clinicaltrials.gov, or contact NIMH.

FOR MORE INFORMATION

National Institute of Mental Health (NIMH)
Office of Communications and Public Liaison
Information Resources and Inquiries
6001 Executive Blvd., Rm. 8184, MSC 9663
Bethesda, MD 20892-9663
Phone: (301) 443-4513; Fax: (301) 443-4279
Fax Back System, Mental Health FAX4U: (301) 443-5158
E-mail: nimhinfo@nih.gov; Web site: http://www.nimh.nih.gov

Child & Adolescent Bipolar Foundation
1187 Wilmette Avenue, PMB #331
Wilmette, IL 60091
Phone: (847) 256-8525
Web site: http://www.bpkids.org

Depression and Related Affective Disorders Association (DRADA)
Johns Hopkins Hospital, Meyer 3-181
600 North Wolfe Street
Baltimore, MD 21287-7381
Phone: (410) 955-4647 or (202) 955-5800 (Wash. D.C.)
E-mail: drada@jhmi.edu; Web site: http://www.drada.org

National Alliance for the Mentally Ill (NAMI)
Colonial Place Three
2107 Wilson Blvd., 3rd
Arlington, VA 22201-3042
Toll-Free: 1-800-950-NAMI (6264)
Phone: (703) 524-7600; Fax: (703) 524-9094
Web site: http://www.nami.org

Depression & Bipolar Support Alliance (DBSA)
730 North Franklin Street, Suite 501
Chicago, IL 60610-7204
Toll-Free: 1-800-826-3632
Phone: (312) 642-0049; Fax: (312) 642-7243
Web site: http://www.DBSAAlliance.org

National Foundation for Depressive Illness, Inc. (NAFDI)
P.O. Box 2257
New York, NY 10116
Toll-Free: 1-800-239-1265
Web site: http://www.depression.org

National Mental Health Association (NMHA)
2001 N Beauregard St, 12th floor
Alexandria, VA 22311
Toll-Free: 1-800-969-NMHA (6642)
Phone: (703) 684-7722; Fax: (703) 684-5968
E-mail: infoctr@nmha.org; Web site: http://www.nmha.org

REFERENCES

[1] Narrow WE (1998). One-year prevalence of depressive disorders among adults 18 and over in the U.S.: NIMH ECA prospective data. Population estimates based on U.S. Census estimated residential population age 18 and over on July 1, 1998. Unpublished.

[2] Regier, DA; Narrow, WE; Rae, DS; et al. (1993). The de facto mental and addictive disorders service system. Epidemiologic Catchment Area prospective 1-year prevalence rates of disorders and services. *Archives of General Psychiatry, 50(2)*: 85-94.

[3]   American Psychiatric Association (1994). *Diagnostic and Statistical Manual for Mental Disorders, fourth edition (DSM-IV)*. Washington, DC: American Psychiatric Press.

[4]   Hyman, SE; Rudorfer, MV (2000). Depressive and bipolar mood disorders. In: Dale DC, Federman DD, eds. *Scientific American*® *Medicine. Vol. 3*. New York: Healtheon/ WebMD Corp., Sect. 13, Subsect. II, p. 1.

[5]   Goodwin, FK & Jamison, KR (1990). *Manic-depressive illness*. New York: Oxford University Press.

[6]   Geller, B & Luby, J (1997). Child and adolescent bipolar disorder: a review of the past 10 years. *Journal of the American Academy of Child and Adolescent Psychiatry*; *36(9)*: 1168-76.

[7]   NIMH Genetics Workgroup (1998). *Genetics and mental disorders*. NIH Publication No. 98-4268. Rockville, MD: National Institute of Mental Health.

[8]   Hyman, SE (1999). Introduction to the complex genetics of mental disorders. *Biological Psychiatry, 45(5)*: 518-21.

[9]   Soares, JC & Mann, JJ (1997). The anatomy of mood disorders—review of structural neuroimaging studies. *Biological Psychiatry, 41(1)*: 86-106.

[10] Soares, JC & Mann, JJ (1997). The functional neuroanatomy of mood disorders. *Journal of Psychiatric Research*, *31(4)*: 393-432.

[11] Sachs, GS; Printz, DJ; Kahn, DA; Carpenter, D & Docherty, JP (2000). The expert consensus guideline series: medication treatment of bipolar disorder 2000. *Postgraduate Medicine,* Spec No:1-104.

[12] Sachs, GS; & Thase ME (2000). Bipolar disorder therapeutics: maintenance treatment. *Biological Psychiatry, 48(6)*: 573-81.

[13] Huxley, NA; Parikh, SV & Baldessarini RJ (2000). Effectiveness of psychosocial treatments in bipolar disorder: state of the evidence. *Harvard Review of Psychiatry, 8(3)*: 126-40.

[14] Vainionpaa LK, Rattya J, Knip M, Tapanainen JS, Pakarinen AJ, Lanning P, Tekay A, Myllyla VV, Isojarvi JI. Valproate-induced hyperandrogenism during pubertal maturation in girls with epilepsy. *Annals of Neurology,* 1999; 45(4): 444-50.

[15] Llewellyn, A; Stowe, ZN & Strader, JR Jr (1998). The use of lithium and management of women with bipolar disorder during pregnancy and lactation. J Clin Psychiatry. *59(Suppl 6):* 57-64; discussion 65.

[16] Thase, ME; Sachs, GS (2000). Bipolar depression: pharmacotherapy and related therapeutic strategies. *Biological Psychiatry, 48(6)*: 558-72.

[17] Suppes, T; Webb, A; Paul, B; Carmody, T; Kraemer, H & Rush, AJ (1999). Clinical outcome in a randomized 1-year trial of clozapine versus

treatment as usual for patients with treatment-resistant illness and a history of mania. *American Journal of Psychiatry, 156(8):* 1164-9.

[18] Tohen, M; Sanger, TM; McElroy, SL; Tollefson, GD; Chengappa, KN; Daniel, DG; Petty F, Centorrino F; Wang R; Grundy, SL; Greaney, MG; Jacobs, TG; David, SR & Toma, V (1999). Olanzapine versus placebo in the treatment of acute mania. Olanzapine HGEH Study Group. *American Journal of Psychiatry, 156(5)*: 702-9.

[19] Rothschild,AJ;Bates,KS; Boehringer, KL & Syed, A (1999). Olanzapine response in psychotic depression. *Journal of Clinical Psychiatry, 60(2)*: 116-8.

[20] U.S. Department of Health and Human Services. (1999). *Mental health: a report of the Surgeon General.* Rockville, MD: U.S. Department of Health and Human Services, Substance Abuse and Mental Health Services Administration, Center for Mental Health Services, National Institutes of Health, National Institute of Mental Health.

[21] Henney, JE (2000). Risk of drug interactions with St. John's wort. From the Food and Drug Administration. *Journal of the American Medical Association, 283(13)*: 1679.

[22] Nierenberg, AA; Burt, T; Matthews, J & Weiss, AP (1999). Mania associated with St. John's wort. *Biological Psychiatry, 46(12):* 1707-8.

[23] Stoll, AL; Severus, WE; Freeman, MP; Rueter, S; Zboyan, HA; Diamond, E; Cress, KK & Marangell, LB (1999). Omega 3 fatty acids in bipolar disorder: a preliminary double-blind, placebo-controlled trial. *Archives of General Psychiatry, 56(5):* 407-12.

[24] Strakowski, SM & DelBello, MP (2000). The co-occurrence of bipolar and substance use disorders. *Clinical Psychology Review, 20(2)*: 191-206.

[25] Mueser, KT; Goodman, LB; Trumbetta, SL; Rosenberg, SD; Osher, FC; Vidaver, R; Auciello, P & Foy, DW (1998). Trauma and posttraumatic stress disorder in severe mental illness. *Journal of Consulting and Clinical Psychology, 66(3)*: 493-9.

[26] Strakowski, SM; Sax, KW; McElroy, SL; Keck, PE Jr; Hawkins, JM & West, SA (1998). Course of psychiatric and substance abuse syndromes co-occurring with bipolar disorder after a first psychiatric hospitalization. *Journal of Clinical Psychiatry, 59(9)*: 465-71.

This publication, written by Melissa Spearing of NIMH, is a revision and update of an earlier version by Mary Lynn Hendrix. Scientific information and review were provided by NIMH Director Steven E. Hyman, M.D., and other NIMH staff members Matthew V. Rudorfer, M.D., and Jane L. Pearson, Ph.D. Editorial assistance was provided by Clarissa K. Wittenberg, Margaret Strock, and Lisa D. Alberts of NIMH.

All material in this booklet is in the public domain and may be copied or reproduced without permission from the Institute. Citation of the source is appreciated.

Addendum to Bipolar
January 2007

Aripiprazole (Abilify) is another atypical antipsychotic medication used to treat the symptoms of schizophrenia and manic or mixed (manic and depressive) episodes of bipolar I disorder. Aripiprazole is in tablet and liquid form. An injectable form is used in the treatment of symptoms of agitation in schizophrenia and manic or mixed episodes of bipolar I disorder.

This is the electronic version of a National Institute of Mental Health (NIMH) publication, available from http://www.nimh.nih.gov/publicat/index.cfm. To order a print copy, call the NIMH Information Center at 301-443-4513 or 1-866-615-6464 (toll-free). Visit the NIMH Web site (http://www.nimh.nih.gov) for information that supplements this publication.

To learn more about NIMH programs and publications, contact the following:

Web address: E-mail: http://www.nimh.nih.govnimhinfo@nih.gov

Phone numbers: 301-443-4513 (local)
Fax numbers: 301-443-4279
1-866-615-6464 (toll-free)301-443-5158 (FAX 4U) 301-443-8431 (TTY)
1-866-415-8051 (TTY toll-free)

Street address:
National Institute of Mental Health
Office of Communications Room 8184, MSC 9663
6001 Executive Boulevard
Bethesda, Maryland 20892-9663 USA

This information is in the public domain and can be copied or reproduced without permission from NIMH. To reference this material, we suggest the following format:

National Institute of Mental Health. Title. Bethesda (MD): National Institute of Mental Health, National Institutes of Health, US Department of Health and Human Services; Year of Publication/Printing [Date of Update/Revision; Date of Citation]. Extent. (NIH Publication No XXX XXXX). Availability.

A specific example is:

National Institute of Mental Health. Childhood-Onset Schizophrenia: An Update from the National Institute of Mental Health. Bethesda (MD): National Institute of Mental Health, National Institutes of Health, US Department of Health and Human Services; 2003 [cited 2004 February 24]. (NIH Publication Number: NIH 5124). 4 pages. Available from: http://www.nimh.nih.gov/publicat/schizkids.cfm.

In: Mental Illness
Editor: Jeremias Koch

ISBN: 978-1-60741-652-4
© 2010 Nova Science Publishers, Inc.

Chapter 2

A STORY OF BIPOLAR DISORDER (MANIC-DEPRESSIVE ILLNESS) DOES THIS SOUND LIKE YOU?

National Institute of Mental Health

Are you feeling really "down" sometimes and really "up" other times? Are these mood changes causing problems at work, school, or home? If yes, you may have **bipolar disorder,** also called **manic-depressive illness.**

JAMES' STORY

"I've had times of feeling "down" and sad most of my life. I used to skip school a lot when I felt like this because I just couldn't get out of bed. At first I didn't take these feelings very seriously.

"I also had times when I felt really terrific, like I could do anything. I felt really "wound up" and I didn't need much sleep. Sometimes friends would tell me I was talking too fast. But everyone around me seemed to be going too slow.

"My job was getting more stressful each week, and the "up" and "down" times were coming more often. My wife and friends said that I was acting very different from my usual self. I kept telling them that everything was fine, there was no problem, and to leave me alone.

"Then, all of a sudden, I couldn't keep it together. I stopped going to work and stayed in bed for days at a time. I felt like my life wasn't worth living anymore. My wife made an appointment for me to see our family doctor and went with me. The doctor checked me out and then sent me to a psychiatrist, who is an expert in treating the kinds of problems I was having.

"The psychiatrist talked with me about how I'd been feeling and acting over the last six months. We also talked about the fact that my grandfather had serious ups and downs like me. I wasn't real familiar with "bipolar disorder," but it sure sounded like what I was going through. It was a great relief to finally know that the ups and downs really were periods of "mania" and "depression" caused by an illness that can be treated.

"For four months now, I've been taking a medicine to keep my moods stable and I see my psychiatrist once a month. I also see someone else for "talk" therapy, which helps me learn how to deal with this illness in my everyday life.

"The first several weeks were hard before the medicine and talk therapy started to work. But now, my mood changes are much less severe and don't happen as often. I'm able to go to work each day, and I'm starting to enjoy things again with my family and friends."

Many people who have bipolar disorder don't know they have it. This booklet can help. It tells you about four steps you can take to understand and get help for bipolar disorder.

FOUR STEPS TO UNDERSTAND AND GET HELP FOR BIPOLAR DISORDER

1. Look for signs of bipolar disorder.
2. Understand that bipolar disorder is a real illness.
3. See your doctor. Get a checkup and talk about how you are feeling.
4. Get treatment for your bipolar disorder. You can feel better.

Step 1. Look for Signs of Bipolar Disorder

Read the following lists. Put a check mark √ by each sign that sounds like you now or in the past:

Signs of mania (ups)

___ I feel like I'm on top of the world.
___ I feel powerful. I can do anything I want, nothing can stop me.
___ I have lots of energy.
___ I don't seem to need much sleep.
___ I feel restless all the time.
___ I feel really mad.
___ I have a lot of sexual energy.
___ I can't focus on anything for very long.
___ I sometimes can't stop talking and I talk really fast.
___ I'm spending lots of money on things I don't need and can't afford.
___ Friends tell me that I've been acting differently. They tell me that I'm starting fights, talking louder, and getting more angry.

Signs of depression (downs)

___ I am really sad most of the time.
___ I don't enjoy doing the things I've always enjoyed doing.
___ I don't sleep well at night and am very restless.
___ I am always tired. I find it hard to get out of bed.
___ I don't feel like eating much.
___ I feel like eating all the time.

___ I have lots of aches and pains that don't go away.

___ I have little to no sexual energy.

___ I find it hard to focus and am very forgetful.

___ I am mad at everybody and everything.

___ I feel upset and fearful, but can't figure out why.

___ I don't feel like talking to people.

___ I feel like there isn't much point to living, nothing good is going to happen to me.

___ I don't like myself very much. I feel bad most of the time.

___ I think about death a lot. I even think about how I might kill myself.

Other signs of bipolar disorder

___ I go back and forth between feeling really "up" and feeling really "down."

___ My ups and downs cause problems at work and at home.

If you checked several boxes in these lists, call your doctor. Take the lists to show your doctor. You may need to get a checkup and find out if you have bipolar disorder.

Step 2 Understand That Bipolar Disorder is a Real Illness

Bipolar disorder is more than the usual ups and downs of life. It is a serious medical illness that involves the brain. The up feelings are called **mania** and the down feelings are called **depression**.

Most people with bipolar disorder go back and forth between mania and depression. Some people have both feelings at the same time, which is called a **mixed** state.

About 5.7 million Americans have bipolar disorder. It can happen to anyone, no matter what age you are or where you come from.

What Causes Bipolar Disorder?

You may want to know why you feel these extreme ups and downs. There may be several causes.

- Bipolar disorder may happen because of changes in your brain.
- Bipolar disorder tends to run in families. This means that someone in your family such as a grandparent, parent, aunt, uncle, cousin, sister, or brother may have bipolar disorder.
- Sometimes the cause of bipolar disorder is not clear.

Bipolar disorder is a serious illness, but it can be treated. You can feel better.

SUICIDE

Sometimes bipolar disorder can cause people to feel like killing themselves. **If you are thinking about killing yourself or know someone who is talking about it, get help:**

- Call 911.
- Go to the emergency room of the nearest hospital.
- Call and talk to your doctor now.
- Ask a friend or family member to take you to the hospital or call your doctor.

Step 3 See Your Doctor

Don't wait. Talk to your doctor about how you are feeling. Get a medical checkup to rule out any other illnesses that might be causing your mood changes. Ask your doctor to send you to a **psychiatrist** (a medical doctor trained in helping people with bipolar disorder).

If you don't have a doctor, check your local phone book. Go to the government services pages (they may be blue in color) and look for "health clinics" or "community health centers." Call one near you and ask for help.

Step 4 Get Treatment for Your Bipolar Disorder. You Can Feel Better.

There are two common types of treatment for bipolar disorder: (1) medicine and (2) "talk" therapy.

Having both kinds of treatment usually works best. It is important to get help because bipolar disorder can get worse without treatment. Bipolar disorder is a long-term illness that needs to be treated throughout a person's lifetime.

Medicine

- See the psychiatrist your doctor suggests. He or she can prescribe medicines that work to control your moods. These medicines are called **"mood stabilizers."** You also may need to take other medicines to help treat your illness.
- The medicines may take a few weeks to work. Be sure to tell your psychiatrist how you are feeling. If you are not feeling better, you may need to try different medicines to find out what works best for you.
- Medicines sometimes cause unwanted "side effects." You may feel tired, have blurred vision, or feel sick to your stomach. Tell your psychiatrist if you have these or any other side effects.

Talk Therapy

- "Talk" therapy involves talking to someone such as a **psychologist, social worker**, or **counselor**. It helps you learn to change how bipolar disorder makes you think, feel, and act. Ask your psychiatrist who you should go to for talk therapy.

You can feel better.

How to Help Someone with Severe Mood Changes

If you know someone who is having severe mood changes and may need help, here are some things you can do:

- Tell the person that you are concerned about him or her.
- Share this booklet with the person.
- Talk to the person about seeing a doctor.
- Take the person to see the doctor.
- If the doctor offers the name and phone number of a psychiatrist or someone for "talk" therapy, call the number and help the person make an appointment.
- Take the person to the appointment.
- "Be there" for the person after he or she starts treatment.
- Contact any of the places listed under "For more information" in this booklet.

For More Information

You can call or write any of these organizations for free information about bipolar disorder. You can also find more information on their web sites. "Free call" phone numbers can be used free by anyone, anywhere in the United States.

National Institute of Mental Health (NIMH)
Office of Communications and Public Liaison
Information Resources and Inquiries Branch
6001 Executive Boulevard
Room 8184, MSC 9663
Bethesda, MD 20892-9663
Free call: 1-800-421-4211
Local call: 301-443-4513
Hearing impaired (TTY): 301-443-8431
Web site: http://www.nimh.nih.gov
E-mail: nimhinfo@nih.gov

National Alliance for the Mentally Ill (NAMI)
2107 Wilson Boulevard, Suite 300
Arlington, VA 22201-3042
Free call: 1-800-950-6264
Local call: 703-524-7600
Web site: http://www.nami.org

National Depressive and Manic Depressive Association (NDMDA)
730 N. Franklin Street, Suite 501
Chicago, IL 60601-7204
Free call: 1-800-826-3632
Local call: 312-642-0049
Web site: http://www.ndmda.org

National Foundation for Depressive Illness, Inc. (NAFDI)
P.O. Box 2257
New York, NY 10116
Free call: 1-800-239-1265
Local call: 212-268-4260
Web site: http://www.depression.org

National Mental Health Association (NMHA)
1021 Prince Street
Alexandria, VA 22314-2971
Free call: 1-800-969-6642
Local call: 703-684-7722
Free call - hearing impaired (TTY): 1-800-433-5959
Web site: http://www.nmha.org
 Child & Adolescent Bipolar Foundation
1187 Willmette Avenue, PMB #331
Willmette, IL 60091
Local call: 847-256-8525
Web site: http://www.bpkids.org

This publication has been adapted by Melissa Spearing, Office of Communications and Public Liaison, National Institute of Mental Health from "Bipolar Disorder," NIH Publication No. 01-3679.

THINGS TO REMEMBER

- Look for signs of bipolar disorder.
- Understand that bipolar disorder is a real illness.
- See your doctor.Get a check-up and talk about how you are feeling.
- Get treatment for your bipolar disorder.You can feel better.

This is the electronic version of a National Institute of Mental Health (NIMH) publication, available from http://www.nimh.nih.gov/publicat/index.cfm. To order a print copy, call the NIMH Information Center at 301-443-4513 or 1-866-615-6464 (toll-free). Visit the NIMH Web site (http://www.nimh.nih.gov) for information that supplements this publication.

To learn more about NIMH programs and publications, contact the following:

Web address:
http://www.nimh.nih.gov

E-mail:
nimhinfo@nih.gov

Phone numbers:
301-443-4513 (local)
1-866-615-6464 (toll-free)
301-443-3431 (TTY)

Fax numbers:
301-443-4279
301-443-5158 (FAX 4U)

Street address:
National Institute of Mental Health
Office of Communications
Room 8184, MSC 9663
6001 Executive Boulevard
Bethesda, Maryland 20892-9663 USA

This information is in the public domain and can be copied or reproduced without permission from NIMH. To reference this material, we suggest the following format:

National Institute of Mental Health. Title. Bethesda (MD): National Institute of Mental Health, National Institutes of Health, US Department of Health and Human Services; Year of Publication/Printing [Date of Update/Revision; Date of Citation]. Extent. (NIH Publication No XXX XXXX). Availability.

A specific example is:

National Institute of Mental Health. Childhood-Onset Schizophrenia: An Update from the National Institute of Mental Health. Bethesda (MD): National Institute of Mental Health, National Institutes of Health, US Department of Health and Human Services; 2003 [cited 2004 February 24]. (NIH Publication Number: NIH 5124). 4 pages. Available from: http://www.nimh.nih.gov/publicat/schizkids.cfm.

In: Mental Illness
Editor: Jeremias Koch

ISBN: 978-1-60741-652-4
© 2010 Nova Science Publishers, Inc.

Chapter 3

COMORBIDITY: ADDICTION AND OTHER MENTAL ILLNESSES

National Institute on Drug Abuse

FROM THE DIRECTOR

Comorbidity is a topic that our stakeholders—patients, family members, health care professionals, and others—frequently ask about. It is also a topic about which we have insufficient information, and so it remains a research priority for NIDA. This Research Report provides information on the state of the science in this area. And although a variety of diseases commonly co-occur with drug abuse and addiction (e.g. HIV, hepatitis C, cancer, cardiovascular disease), this report focuses only on the comorbidity of drug use disorders and other mental illnesses.*

To help explain this comorbidity, we need to first recognize that drug addiction is a mental illness. It is a complex brain disease characterized by compulsive, at times uncontrollable drug craving, seeking, and use despite devastating consequences—behaviors that stem from drug-induced changes in brain structure and function. These changes occur in some of the same brain areas that are disrupted in various other mental disorders, such as depression, anxiety, or schizophrenia. It is therefore not surprising that population surveys show a high rate of co-occurrence, or comorbidity, between drug addiction and other mental illnesses. Even though we cannot always prove a connection or causality, we do know that certain mental disorders are established risk factors for subsequent drug abuse—and vice versa.

It is often difficult to disentangle the overlapping symptoms of drug addiction and other mental illnesses, making diagnosis and treatment complex. Correct diagnosis is critical to ensuring appropriate and effective treatment. Ignorance of or failure to treat a comorbid disorder can jeopardize a patient's chance of success. We hope that our enhanced understanding of the common genetic, environmental, and neural bases of these disorders—and the dissemination of this information—will lead to improved treatments for comorbidity and will diminish the social stigma that makes patients reluctant to seek the treatment they need.

Nora D. Volkow, M.D., Director
National Institute on Drug Abuse

WHAT IS COMORBIDITY?

When two disorders or illnesses occur in the same person, simultaneously or sequentially, they are called comorbid. Comorbidity also implies interactions between the illnesses that affect the course and prognosis of both.

IS DRUG ADDICTION A MENTAL ILLNESS?

Yes, because addiction changes the brain in fundamental ways, disturbing a person's normal hierarchy of needs and desires and substituting new priorities connected with procuring and using the drug. The resulting compulsive behaviors that override the ability to control impulses despite the consequences are similar to hallmarks of other mental illnesses.

In fact, the *Diagnostic and Statistical Manual of Mental Disorders* (DSM), the definitive resource of diagnostic criteria for all mental disorders, includes criteria for *drug use disorders*, distinguishing between two types: drug abuse and drug dependence. *Drug dependence* is synonymous with addiction. By comparison, the criteria for *drug abuse* hinge on the harmful consequences of repeated use but do not include the compulsive use, tolerance (i.e., needing higher doses to achieve the same effect), or withdrawal (i.e., symptoms that occur when use is stopped) that can be signs of addiction.

Addiction changes the brain, disturbing the normal hierarchy of needs and desires.

CHILDHOOD ADHD AND LATER DRUG PROBLEMS

Numerous studies have documented an increased risk for drug use disorders in youth with untreated ADHD, although some suggest that only a subset of these individuals are vulnerable: those with comorbid conduct disorders. Given this linkage, it is important to determine whether effective treatment of ADHD could prevent subsequent drug abuse and associated behavioral problems. Treatment of childhood ADHD with stimulant medications such as methylphenidate or amphetamine reduces the impulsive behavior, fidgeting, and inability to concentrate that characterize ADHD. However, some physicians and parents have expressed concern that treating childhood ADHD with stimulants might increase a child's vulnerability to drug abuse later in life. Recent reviews of long-term studies of children with ADHD who received stimulant therapy found no evidence for this increase. However, most of these studies have methodological limitations, including small sample sizes and non-randomized study designs, indicating that more research is needed, particularly in adolescents.

HOW COMMON ARE COMORBID DRUG USE AND OTHER MENTAL DISORDERS?

Many people who regularly abuse drugs are also diagnosed with mental disorders and vice versa. The high prevalence of this comorbidity has been documented in multiple national population surveys since the 1980s. Data show that persons diagnosed with mood or anxiety disorders were about twice as likely to suffer also from a drug use disorder (abuse or dependence) compared with respondents in general. The same was true for those diagnosed with an antisocial syndrome, such as antisocial personality or conduct disorder. Similarly, persons diagnosed with drug disorders were roughly twice as likely to suffer also from mood and anxiety disorders (see page 3, "Overlapping Conditions—Shared Vulnerability").

Gender is also a factor in the specific patterns of observed comorbidities. For example, the overall rates of abuse and dependence for most drugs tend to be higher among males than females, and males are more likely to suffer also from antisocial personality disorder. In contrast, women have higher rates of amphetamine dependence and higher rates of mood and anxiety disorders.

Overlapping Conditions—Shared Vulnerability

Because mood disorders increase vulnerability to drug abuse and addiction, the diagnosis and treatment of the mood disorder can reduce the risk of subsequent drug use. Because the inverse may also be true, the diagnosis and treatment of drug use disorders may reduce the risk of developing other mental illnesses and, if they do occur, lessen their severity or make them more amenable to effective treatment. Finally, because more than 40 percent of the cigarettes smoked in this country are smoked by individuals with a psychiatric disorder, such as major depressive disorder; alcoholism; post-traumatic stress disorder (PTSD); schizophrenia; or bipolar disorder, smoking by patients with mental illness contributes greatly to their increased morbidity and mortality.

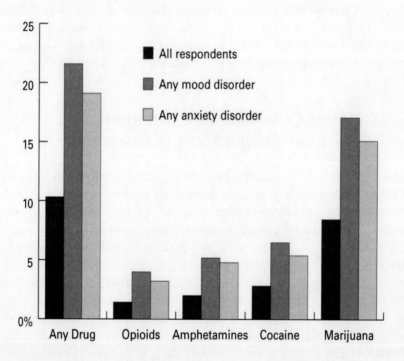

High Prevalence of Drug Abuse and Dependence Among Individuals With Mood and Anxiety Disorders

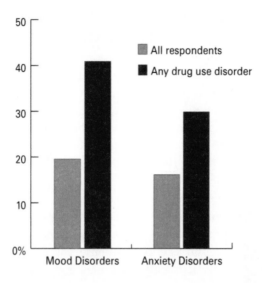

Higher Prevalence of Mental Disorders among Patients with Drug Use Disorders

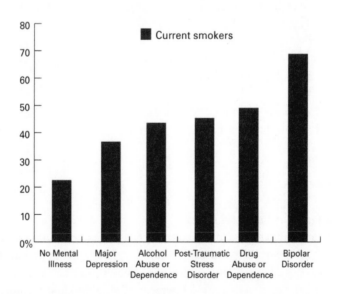

Higher Prevalence Smoking among Patients with Mental Disorders

Data in top two graphs reprinted from the National Epidemiologic Survey on Alcohol and Related Conditions (Conway et al., 2006). Data in bottom graph from the 1989 U.S. National Health Interview Survey (Lasser et al., 2000).

WHY DO DRUG USE DISORDERS OFTEN CO-OCCUR WITH OTHER MENTAL ILLNESSES?

The high prevalence of comorbidity between drug use disorders and other mental illnesses does not mean that one caused the other, even if it appeared first. In fact, establishing causality or directionality is difficult for several reasons. Some symptoms of a mental disorder may not be recognized until the illness has substantially progressed, and imperfect recollections of when drug use/abuse started can also present timing issues. Still, three scenarios deserve consideration:

1. Drugs of abuse can cause abusers to experience one or more symptoms of another mental illness. The increased risk of psychosis in some marijuana abusers has been offered as evidence for this possibility.
2. Mental illnesses can lead to drug abuse. Individuals with overt, mild, or even subclinical mental disorders may abuse drugs as a form of self-medication. For example, the use of tobacco products by patients with schizophrenia is believed to lessen the symptoms of the disease and improve cognition (see page 4, "Smoking and Schizophrenia: Self-Medication or Shared Brain Circuitry?").
3. Both drug use disorders and other mental illnesses are caused by over-lapping factors such as underlying brain deficits, genetic vulnerabilities, and/or early exposure to stress or trauma.

All three scenarios probably contribute, in varying degrees, to how and whether specific comorbidities manifest themselves.

Common Factors

Overlapping Genetic Vulnerabilities
A particularly active area of comorbidity research involves the search for *genes* that might predispose individuals to develop both addiction and other mental illnesses, or to have a greater risk of a second disorder occurring after the first appears. It is estimated that 40–60 percent of an individual's vulnerability to addiction is attributable to genetics; most of this vulnerability arises from complex interactions among multiple genes and from genetic interactions with environmental influences. In some instances, a gene product may act directly, as when a protein influences how a person responds to a drug (e.g., whether the drug

experience is pleasurable or not) or how long a drug remains in the body. But genes can also act indirectly by altering how an individual responds to stress or by increasing the likelihood of risk-taking and novelty-seeking behaviors, which could influence the development of both drug use disorders and other mental illnesses. Several regions of the human genome have been linked to increased risk of both, including associations with greater vulnerability to adolescent drug dependence and conduct disorders.

Involvement of Similar Brain Regions

Some areas of the brain are affected by both drug use disorders and other mental illnesses. For example, the circuits in the brain that use the neurotransmitter dopamine—a chemical that carries messages from one neuron to another—are typically affected by addictive substances and may also be involved in depression, schizophrenia, and other psychiatric disorders. Indeed, some antidepressants and essentially all antipsychotic medications target the regulation of dopamine in this system directly, whereas others may have indirect effects. Importantly, dopamine pathways have also been implicated in the way in which stress can increase vulnerability to drug addiction. Stress is also a known risk factor for a range of mental disorders and therefore provides one likely common neurobiological link between the disease processes of addiction and those of other mental disorders.

The overlap of brain areas involved in both drug use disorders and other mental illnesses suggests that brain changes stemming from one may affect the other. For example, drug abuse that precedes the first symptoms of a mental illness may produce changes in brain structure and function that kindle an underlying propensity to develop that mental illness. If the mental disorder develops first, associated changes in brain activity may increase the vulnerability to abusing substances by enhancing their positive effects, reducing awareness of their negative effects, or alleviating the unpleasant effects associated with the mental disorder or the medication used to treat it.

The Influence of Developmental Stage

Adolescence—A Vulnerable Time

Although drug abuse and addiction can happen at any time during a person's life, drug *use* typically starts in adolescence, a period when the first signs of mental illness commonly appear. It is therefore not surprising that comorbid disorders can already be seen among youth. Significant changes in the brain occur during adolescence, which may enhance vulnerability to drug use and the development of addiction and other mental disorders. Drugs of abuse affect brain circuits involved in reward, decisionmaking, learning and memory, and behavioral control, all of which are still maturing into early adulthood. Thus, understanding the long-term impact of early drug exposure is a critical area of comorbidity research.

Early Occurrence Increases Later Risk

Strong evidence has emerged showing early drug use to be a risk factor for later substance abuse problems; additional findings suggest that it may also be a risk factor for the later occurrence of other mental illnesses. However, this link is not necessarily a simple one and may hinge upon genetic vulnerability, psychosocial experiences, and/or general environmental influences. A recent study highlights this complexity, with the finding that frequent marijuana use during adolescence can increase the risk of psychosis in adulthood, but only in individuals who carry a particular gene variant (see sidebar, "The Influence of Adolescent Marijuana Use on Adult Psychosis Is Affected by Genetic Variables").

It is also true that having a mental disorder in childhood or adolescence can increase the risk of later drug abuse problems, as frequently occurs with conduct disorder and untreated attention-deficit hyperactivity disorder (ADHD). This presents a challenge when treating children with ADHD, since effective treatment often involves prescribing stimulant medications with abuse potential. This issue has generated strong interest from the research community, and although the results are not yet conclusive, most studies suggest that ADHD medications do not increase the risk of drug abuse among children with ADHD (see page 2, "Childhood ADHD and Later Drug Problems").

Regardless of how comorbidity develops, it is common in youth as well as adults. Given the high prevalence of comorbid mental disorders and their likely adverse impact on substance abuse treatment outcomes, drug abuse programs for adolescents should include screening and, if needed, treatment for comorbid mental disorders.

The high rate of comorbidity between drug abuse and addiction and other mental disorders argues for a comprehensive approach to intervention that identifies, evaluates, and treats each disorder concurrently.

SMOKING AND SCHIZOPHRENIA: SELF-MEDICATION OR SHARED BRAIN CIRCUITRY?

Patients with schizophrenia have higher rates of alcohol, tobacco, and other drug abuse than the general population. Based on nationally representative survey data, 41 percent of respondents with past-month mental illnesses are current smokers, which is about double the rate of those with no mental illness. In clinical samples, the rate of smoking in patients with schizophrenia has ranged as high as 90 percent.

Various self-medication hypotheses have been proposed to explain the strong association between schizophrenia and smoking, although none have yet been confirmed. Most of these relate to the nicotine contained in tobacco products: Nicotine may help compensate for some of the cognitive impairments produced by the disorder and may counteract psychotic symptoms or alleviate unpleasant side effects of antipsychotic medications. Nicotine or smoking behavior may also help people with schizophrenia deal with the anxiety and social stigma of their disease.

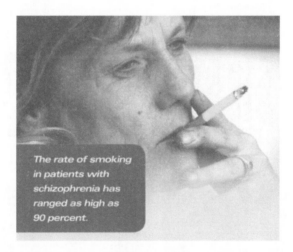

The rate of smoking in patients with schizophrenia has ranged as high as 90 percent.

Research on how both nicotine and schizophrenia affect the brain has generated other possible explanations for the high rate of smoking among people with schizophrenia: The presence of abnormalities in particular circuits of the brain may predispose individuals to schizophrenia; increase the rewarding effects of drugs **like nicotine; or reduce an individual's ability to quit smoking. The** involvement of common mechanisms is consistent with the observation that both nicotine and the medication clozapine (which also acts at nicotine receptors) can improve attention and working memory in an animal model of schizophrenia. Clozapine is effective in treating individuals with schizophrenia. It also reduces their smoking levels. Understanding how and why patients with schizophrenia use nicotine is likely to help us develop new treatments for both schizophrenia and nicotine dependence.

THE BRAIN CONTINUES TO DEVELOP INTO ADULTHOOD AND UNDERGOES DRAMATIC CHANGES DURING ADOLESCENCE

One of the brain areas still maturing during adolescence is the prefrontal cortex—the part of the brain that enables us to assess situations, make sound decisions, and keep our emotions and desires under control. The fact that this critical part of an adolescent's brain is still a work in progress puts them at increased risk for poor decisions (such as trying drugs or continuing abuse). Thus, introducing drugs while the brain is still developing may have profound and long-lasting consequences.

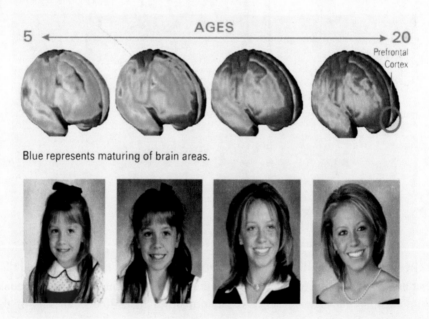

Blue represents maturing of brain areas.

THE INFLUENCE OF ADOLESCENT MARIJUANA USE ON ADULT PSYCHOSIS IS AFFECTED BY GENETIC VARIABLES

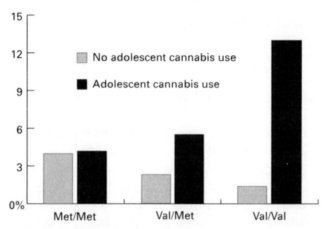

Source: Caspi A, Moffitt TE, Cannon M, et al., 2005.

Percentage of Individuals Meeting Diagnostic Criteria for Schizophreniform Disorder at Age 26.

The above figure shows that variations in a gene can affect the likelihood of developing psychosis in adulthood following exposure to cannabis. The Catechol-O-Methyltransferase gene regulates an enzyme that breaks down dopamine, a brain chemical involved in schizophrenia. It comes in two forms: Met and Val. Individuals with one or two copies of the Val variant have a higher risk of developing schizophrenic-type disorders if they used cannabis during adolescence (dark bars). Those with only the Met variant were unaffected by cannabis use. These findings hint at the complexity of factors that contribute to comorbid conditions; however, more research is needed.

HOW CAN COMORBIDITY BE DIAGNOSED?

The high rate of comorbidity between drug use disorders and other mental illnesses argues for a comprehensive approach to intervention that identifies, evaluates, and treats each disorder concurrently. The needed approach calls for broad assessment tools that are less likely to result in a missed diagnosis. Accordingly, patients entering treatment for psychiatric illnesses should also be screened for substance use disorders and vice versa. Accurate diagnosis is complicated, however, by the similarities between drug-related symptoms such as withdrawal and those of potentially comorbid mental disorders. Thus, when people who abuse drugs enter treatment, it may be necessary to observe them after a period of abstinence in order to distinguish the effects of substance intoxication or withdrawal from the symptoms of comorbid mental disorders—this would allow for a more accurate diagnosis.

HOW SHOULD COMORBID CONDITIONS BE TREATED?

A fundamental principle emerging from scientific research is the need to treat comorbid conditions concurrently—which can be a difficult proposition (see page **9, "Barriers to Comprehensive Treatment of Comorbidity"**). Patients who have both a drug use disorder and another mental illness often exhibit symptoms that are more persistent, severe, and resistant to treatment compared with patients who have either disorder alone. Nevertheless, steady progress is being made through research on new and existing treatment options for comorbidity and through health services research on implementation of appropriate screening and treatment within a variety of settings (e.g., NIDA's Criminal Justice Drug Abuse Treatment Studies [CJ-DATS]).

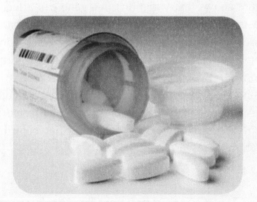

Medications

Effective medications exist for treating opioid, alcohol, and nicotine addiction and for alleviating the symptoms of many other mental disorders. Most of these medications have not been studied in patients with comorbidities, although some may prove effective for treating comorbid conditions. For example, preliminary results of a recent study point to the potential of using divalproex (trade name: Depakote)—an anticonvulsant commonly used to treat bipolar disorder—to treat patients with comorbid bipolar disorder and primary cocaine dependence. Other evidence suggests that bupropion (trade names: Wellbutrin, Zyban), approved for treating depression and nicotine dependence, might also help reduce craving and use of methamphetamine. Most medications have not been well studied in comorbid populations or in populations taking other psychoactive medications. Therefore, more research is needed to fully understand and assess the actions of combined or dually effective medications.

Behavioral Therapies

Behavioral treatment (alone or in combination with medications) is the cornerstone to successful outcomes for many individuals with drug use disorders or other mental illnesses. And while behavior therapies continue to be evaluated for use in comorbid populations, several strategies have shown promise for treating specific comorbid conditions (see page 8, "Examples of Promising Behavioral Therapies for Patients With Comorbid Conditions").

Most clinicians and researchers agree that broad spectrum diagnosis and concurrent therapy will lead to more positive outcomes for patients with comorbid conditions. Preliminary findings support this notion, but research is needed to identify the most effective therapies (especially studies focused on adolescents).

EXPOSURE TO TRAUMATIC EVENTS PUTS PEOPLE AT HIGHER RISK OF SUBSTANCE USE DISORDERS

Emotionally traumatized people are at much higher risk of abusing licit, illicit, and prescription drugs. The strong association between PTSD and substance abuse is particularly frequent and devastating among military veterans, among whom 38,000 PTSD cases have been documented in the past 5 years alone. Epidemiological studies suggest that as many as half of them may have a co-occurring substance use disorder (SUD). The growing incidence of PTSD among returning veterans poses an enormous challenge for a health care system in which PTSD programs don't accept individuals with active SUDs while traditional SUD clinics defer the treatment of trauma-related issues. However, there are treatment options for PTSD and SUD at different stages of clinical validation; these include various combinations of psychosocial (e.g., exposure therapy) and pharmacologic (e.g., mood stabilizers, antianxiolitics, and antidepressants) interventions. However, more research is urgently needed to identify the best treatment strategies for addressing PTSD comorbidities, in particular depression and SUD, and to explore the notion that different treatments might be needed in response to civilian vs. combat PTSD.

EXAMPLES OF PROMISING BEHAVIORAL THERAPIES FOR PATIENTS WITH COMORBID CONDITIONS

Adolescents

Multisystemic Therapy (MST)
MST targets key factors (attitudes, family, peer pressure, school and neighborhood culture) associated with serious antisocial behavior in children and adolescents who abuse drugs.

Brief Strategic Family Therapy (BSFT)
BSFT targets family interactions that are thought to maintain or exacerbate adolescent drug abuse and other co-occurring problem behaviors. These problem behaviors include conduct problems at home and at school, oppositional behavior, delinquency, associating with antisocial peers, aggressive and violent behavior, and risky sexual behaviors.

Cognitive-Behavioral Therapy (CBT)

CBT is designed to modify harmful beliefs and maladaptive behaviors. CBT is the most effective psychotherapy for children and adolescents with anxiety and mood disorders, and also shows strong efficacy for substance abusers. (CBT is also effective for adult populations suffering from drug use disorders and a range of other psychiatric problems.)

Adults

Therapeutic Communities (TCs)

TCs focus on the "resocialization" of the individual and use broad-based community programs as active components of treatment. TCs are particularly well suited to deal with criminal justice inmates, individuals with vocational deficits, women who need special protections from harsh social environments, vulnerable or neglected youth, and homeless individuals. In addition, some evidence suggests the utility of incorporating TCs for adolescents who have been in treatment for substance   abuse and related problems.

Assertive Community Treatment (ACT)

ACT programs integrate the behavioral treatment of other severe mental disorders, such as schizophrenia, and co-occurring substance use disorders. ACT is differentiated from other forms of case management through factors such as a smaller caseload size, team management, outreach emphasis, a highly individualized approach, and an assertive approach to maintaining contact with patients.

Dialectical Behavior Therapy (DBT)

DBT is designed specifically to reduce self-harm behaviors (such as self-mutilation and suicidal attempts, thoughts, or urges) and drug abuse. It is one of the few treatments that are effective for individuals who meet the criteria for borderline personality disorder.

Exposure Therapy

Exposure therapy is a behavioral treatment for some anxiety disorders (phobias, post-traumatic stress disorder [PTSD]) that involves repeated exposure to or confrontation with a feared situation, object, traumatic event, or memory. This exposure can be real, visualized, or simulated, and always is contained in a controlled therapeutic environment. The goal is to desensitize patients to the triggering stimuli and help them learn to cope, eventually reducing or even eliminating symptoms. Several studies suggest that exposure therapy may be helpful for individuals with comorbid PTSD and cocaine addiction, although retention in treatment is difficult.

Integrated Group Therapy (IGT)

IGT is a new treatment developed specifically for patients with bipolar disorder and drug addiction, designed to address both problems simultaneously.

BARRIERS TO COMPREHENSIVE TREATMENT OF COMORBIDITY

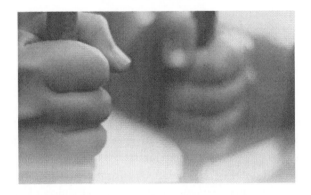

Although research supports the need for comprehensive treatment to address comorbidity, provision of such treatment can be problematic for a number of reasons:

- In the United States different treatment systems address drug use disorders and other mental illnesses separately. Physicians are most often the front line of treatment for mental disorders, whereas drug abuse treatment is provided in assorted venues by a mix of health care professionals with different backgrounds. Thus, neither system may have sufficiently broad expertise to address the full range of problems presented by patients. People also use these health care systems differently, depending on insurance coverage and social factors. For example, when suffering from substance abuse and mental illness comorbidities, women more often pursue treatment services for mental health problems, whereas men tend to seek help through substance abuse treatment channels.
- A lingering bias remains in some substance abuse treatment centers against using any medications, including those necessary to treat serious mental disorders such as depression. Additionally, many substance abuse treatment programs do not employ professionals qualified to prescribe, dispense, and monitor medications.

- Many of those needing treatment are in the criminal justice system. It is estimated that about 75 percent of offenders in State and local prisons and jails have a mental health problem comorbid with substance abuse or addiction. However, adequate treatment services for both drug use disorders and other mental illnesses are greatly lacking within these settings. While treatment provision may be burdensome for the criminal justice system, it offers an opportunity to positively affect the public's health and safety. Treatment of comorbid disorders can reduce not only associated medical complications, but also negative social outcomes by mitigating against a return to criminal behavior and reincarceration.

GLOSSARY

Addiction: A chronic, relapsing disease characterized by compulsive drug seeking and abuse in spite of known adverse consequences, and by functional, sometimes long-lasting changes in the brain.

Antisocial Personality Disorder: A disorder characterized by antisocial behaviors that involve pervasive disregard for and violation of the rights, feelings, and safety of others, beginning in childhood or the early teenage years and continuing into adulthood.

Attention-Deficit Hyperactivity Disorder (ADHD): A disorder characterized by inattentiveness and/or hyperactivity and impulsivity at a level far greater than others of the same age.

Anxiety Disorders: Varied disorders that involve excessive or inappropriate feelings of anxiety or worry. Examples are panic disorder, post-traumatic stress disorder, social phobia, and others.

Bipolar Disorder: A mood disorder characterized by alternating episodes of depression and mania or hypo-mania.

Comorbidity: The occurrence of two disorders or illnesses in the same person, either at the same time (co-occurring comorbid conditions) or with a time difference between the initial occurrence of one and the initial occurrence of the other (sequentially comorbid conditions).

Dopamine: A chemical (neurotransmitter) found in parts of the brain responsible for reward, motivation, and movement.

Dual Diagnosis/Mentally Ill Chemical Abuser (MICA): Other terms used to describe the comorbidity of a drug use disorder and another mental illness.

Depression: A disorder marked by sadness, inactivity, difficulty with thinking and concentration, significant increase or decrease in appetite and time spent sleeping, feelings of dejection and hopelessness, and sometimes, suicidal thoughts or an attempt to commit suicide.

Major Depressive Disorder: A mood disorder having a clinical course of one or more serious depression episodes that last 2 or more weeks. Episodes are characterized by a loss of interest or pleasure in almost all activities; disturbances in appetite, sleep, or psychomotor functioning; a decrease in energy; difficulties in thinking or making decisions; loss of self-esteem or feelings of guilt; and suicidal thoughts or attempts.

Mania: A mood disorder characterized by abnormally and persistently elevated, expansive, or irritable mood; mental and physical hyperactivity; and/or disorganization of behavior.

Mental Disorder: A mental condition marked primarily by sufficient disorganization of personality, mind, and emotions to seriously impair the normal psychological or behavioral functioning of the individual. Addiction is a mental disorder.

Neurotransmitters: The brain's chemical messengers used to transmit information between neurons.

Post-Traumatic Stress Disorder (PTSD): A disorder that develops after exposure to a highly stressful event (e.g., wartime combat, physical violence, or natural disaster). Symptoms include re-experiencing the trauma through flashbacks or recurrent nightmares, hypervigilance and difficulty sleeping, and avoidance of reminders of the event.

Psychosis: A serious mental disorder (e.g., schizophrenia) characterized by defective or lost contact with reality. Symptoms often include hallucinations or delusions.

Schizophrenia: A psychotic disorder characterized by symptoms that fall into two categories: (1) positive symptoms, such as distortions in thoughts (delusions), perception (hallucinations), and language and thinking and (2) negative symptoms, such as flattened emotional responses and decreased goal-directed behavior.

Self-Medication: The use of a substance to lessen the negative effects of stress, anxiety, or other mental disorders (or side effects of their pharmacotherapy). Self-medication may lead to addiction and other drug- or alcohol-related problems.

REFERENCES

Biederman, J., Monuteaux, M. C., Spencer, T., Wilens, T. E., Macpherson, H. A. & Faraone, S. V. (2008). Stimulant therapy and risk for subsequent substance use disorders in male adults with ADHD: A naturalistic controlled 10-year follow up study. *Am J Psychiatry 165(5)*:597–603.

Brady, K. T. & Verduin, M. L. (2005). Pharmaco-therapy of comorbid mood, anxiety, and substance use disorders. *Subst Use Misuse 40*:2021–2041, 2043–2048.

Caspi, A., Moffitt, T. E., Cannon, M., et al. (2005). Moderation of the effect of adolescent-onset cannabis use on adult psychosis by a functional polymorphism in the catechol-O-methyltransferase gene: Longitudinal evidence of a gene x environment interaction. *Biol Psychiatry 57(10)*:1117–1127.

Conway, K. P., Compton, W., Stinson, F. S. & Grant, B. F. (2006). Lifetime comorbidity of DSM-IV mood and anxiety disorders and specific drug use disorders: Results from the National Epidemiologic Survey on Alcohol and Related Conditions. *J Clin Psychiatry 67(2)*:247–257.

Compton, W. M., Conway, K. P., Stinson, F. S., Colliver, J. D. & Grant, B. F. (2005). Prevalence, correlates, and comorbidity of DSM-IV antisocial personality syndromes and alcohol and specific drug use disorders in the United States: Results from the National Epidemiologic Survey on Alcohol and Related Conditions. *J Clin Psychiatry 66(6)*:677–685.

James, D. J. & Glaze, E. (2006). Mental health problems of prison and jail inmates. *Bureau of Justice Statistics Special Report.* NCJ 213600, Washington, DC: U.S. Department of Justice, Bureau of Justice Statistics.

Kessler, R. C. (2004). The epidemiology of dual diagnosis. *Biol Psychiatry 56*:730–737.

Lasser, K, Boyd, J. W., Woolhandler, S., Himmelstein, D. U., McCormick, D. & Bor, D. H. (2000). Smoking and mental illness: A population-based prevalence study. *JAMA 284(20)*:2606–2610.

Mannuzza, S., Klein, R. G., Truong, N. L., Moulton J. L. 3rd, Roizen, E. R., Howell, K. H. & Castellanos, F. X. (2008). Age of methylphenidate treatment initiation in children with ADHD and later substance abuse: Prospective follow-up into adulthood. *Am J Psychiatry 165(5)*:604-609.

Negrete, J. C. (2003). Clinical aspects of substance abuse in persons with schizophrenia. *Can J Psychiatry 48(1)*:14–21.

Nestler, E. J. & Carlezon, W. A., Jr. (2006). The mesolimbic dopamine reward circuit in depression. *Biol Psychiatry 59(12)*: 1151–1159.

Quello, S. B., Brady, K. T. & Sonne, S. C. (2005). Mood disorders and substance abuse disorders: A complex comorbidity. *Science & Practice Perspectives 3(1)*:13–24.

Riggs, P. D. (2003). Treating adolescents for substance abuse and comorbid psychiatric disorders. *Science & Practice Perspectives 2(1)*:18–28.

Saal D, Dong Y, Bonci A, Malenka RC. Drugs of abuse and stress trigger a common synaptic adaptation in dopamine neurons. *Neuron* 37(4): 577–582, 2003.

Uhl, G. R. & Grow, R. W. (2004). The burden of complex genetics in brain disorders. *Arch Gen Psychiatry 61(3)*:223–229.

Volkow, N. D. (2004). The reality of comorbidity: Depression and drug abuse. *Biol Psychiatry 56(10)*:714–717.

Volkow, N. D. & Li, T-K. (2004). Drug addiction: The neurobiology of behavior gone awry. *Nat Rev Neurosc 5(12)*:963–970.

Weiss, R. D., Griffin, M. L., Kolodziej, M. E., et al. (2007). A randomized trial of integrated group therapy versus group drug counseling for patients with bipolar disorder and substance dependence. *Am J Psychiatry 164(1)*:100–107.

Wilens, T. E., Faraone, S. V., Biederman, J. & Gunawardene, S. (2003). Does stimulant therapy of attention-deficit/hyperactivity disorder beget later substance abuse? A meta-analytic review of the literature. *Pediatrics 111(1)*:179–185.

WHERE CAN I GET MORE SCIENTIFIC INFORMATION ON COMORBID ADDICTION AND OTHER MENTAL ILLNESSES?

To learn more about drug use disorders and other mental illnesses, or to order materials on these topics free of charge in English or Spanish, visit the NIDA Web site at www.drugabuse.gov or contact the *DrugPubs* Research Dissemination Center   at 877-NIDA-NIH (877-643-2644; TTY/TDD: 240-645-0228).

What's New on the NIDA Web Site

- Information on drugs of abuse
- Publications and communications (including *NIDA Notes* and *Addiction Science & Clinical Practice* journal)
- Calendar of events
- Links to NIDA organizational units
- Funding information (including program announcements and deadlines)
- International activities
- Links to related Web sites (access to Web sites of many other organizations in the field)

NIDA Web Sites

drugabuse.gov
backtoschool.drugabuse.gov
smoking.drugabuse.gov
hiv.drugabuse.gov
marijuana-info.org
clubdrugs.gov
steroidabuse.gov
teens.drugabuse.gov
inhalants.drugabuse.gov

Other Web Sites

Information on drug abuse and other mental illnesses is also available through these other Web sites:

- National Institute of Mental Health: www.nimh.nih.gov
- National Institute on Alcohol Abuse and Alcoholism: www.niaaa.nih.gov
- Substance Abuse and Mental Health Services Administration Health Information Network: www.samhsa.gov/shin

End Notes

[*] Drug abuse and drug dependence, or addiction, are considered drug use disorders—a subgroup of mental disorders—when they meet the diagnostic criteria delineated in the *Diagnostic and Statistical Manual of Mental Disorders* (DSM). Drug dependence, as DSM defines it, is synonymous with the term "addiction," which will be used preferentially in this report. Since the focus of this report is on comorbid drug use disorders and other mental illnesses, the terms "mental illness"/"mental disorders" will refer here to disorders other than substance use, such as depression, schizophrenia, anxiety, and mania. The terms "dual diagnosis," "mentally ill chemical abuser," and "co-occurrence" are also used to refer to drug use disorders that are comorbid with other mental illnesses.

In: Mental Illness
Editor: Jeremias Koch

ISBN: 978-1-60741-652-4
© 2010 Nova Science Publishers, Inc.

Chapter 4

SCHIZOPHRENIA

National Institute of Mental Health

WHAT IS SCHIZOPHRENIA?

Schizophrenia is a chronic, severe, and disabling brain disorder that has been recognized throughout recorded history. It affects about 1 percent of Americans.[1]

People with schizophrenia may hear voices other people don't hear or they may believe that others are reading their minds, controlling their thoughts, or plotting to harm them. These experiences are terrifying and can cause fearfulness, withdrawal, or extreme agitation. People with schizophrenia may not make sense when they talk, may sit for hours without moving or talking much, or may seem perfectly fine until they talk about what they are really thinking. Because many people with schizophrenia have difficulty holding a job or caring for themselves, the burden on their families and society is significant as well.

Available treatments can relieve many of the disorder's symptoms, but most people who have schizophrenia must cope with some residual symptoms as long as they live. Nevertheless, this is a time of hope for people with schizophrenia and their families. Many people with the disorder now lead rewarding and meaningful lives in their communities. Researchers are developing more effective medications and using new research tools to understand the causes of schizophrenia and to find ways to prevent and treat it.

This brochure presents information on the symptoms of schizophrenia, when the symptoms appear, how the disease develops, current treatments, support for patients and their loved ones, and new directions in research.

WHAT ARE THE SYMPTOMS OF SCHIZOPHRENIA?

The symptoms of schizophrenia fall into three broad categories:

- **Positive symptoms** are unusual thoughts or perceptions, including hallucina-tions, delusions, thought disorder, and disorders of movement.
- **Negative symptoms** represent a loss or a decrease in the ability to initiate plans, speak, express emotion, or find pleasure in everyday life. These symptoms are harder to recognize as part of the disorder and can be mistaken for laziness or depression.

- **Cognitive symptoms** (or cognitive deficits) are problems with attention, certain types of memory, and the executive functions that allow us to plan and organize. Cognitive deficits can also be difficult to recognize as part of the disorder but are the most disabling in terms of leading a normal life.

Positive Symptoms

Positive symptoms are easy-to-spot behaviors not seen in healthy people and usually involve a loss of contact with reality. They include hallucinations, delusions, thought disor-der, and disorders of movement. Positive symptoms can come and go. Sometimes they are severe and at other times hardly noticeable, depending on whether the individual is receiving treatment.

Hallucinations

A hallucination is something a person sees, hears, smells, or feels that no one else can see, hear, smell, or feel. "Voices" are the most common type of hallucination in schizophrenia. Many people with the disorder hear voices that may comment on their behavior, order them to do things, warn them of impending danger, or talk to each other (usually about the patient).They may hear these voices for a long time before family and friends notice that something is wrong. Other types of hallucinations include seeing people or objects that are not there, smelling odors that no one else detects (although this can also be a symptom of certain brain tumors), and feeling things like invisible fingers touching their bodies when no one is near.

Delusions

Delusions are false personal beliefs that are not part of the person's culture and do not change, even when other people present proof that the beliefs are not true or logical. People with schizophrenia can have delusions that are quite bizarre, such as believing that neighbors can control their behavior with magnetic waves, people on television are directing special messages to them, or radio stations are broadcasting their thoughts aloud to others. They may also have delusions of grandeur and think they are famous historical figures. People with paranoid schizophrenia can believe that others are deliberately cheating, harassing, poisoning, spying upon, or plotting against them or the people they care about. These beliefs are called delusions of persecution.

Thought Disorder

People with schizophrenia often have unusual thought processes. One dramatic form is disorganized thinking, in which the person has difficulty organizing his or her thoughts or connecting them logically. Speech may be garbled or hard to understand. Another form is "thought blocking," in which the person stops abruptly in the middle of a thought.When asked why, the person may say that it felt as if the thought had been taken out of his or her head. Finally, the individual might make up unintelligible words, or "neologisms."

Disorders of Movement

People with schizophrenia can be clumsy and uncoordinated.They may also exhibit involuntary movements and may grimace or exhibit unusual mannerisms. They may repeat certain motions over and over or, in extreme cases, may become catatonic. Catatonia is a state of immobility and unresponsiveness. It was more common when treatment for schizophrenia was not available; fortu-nately, it is now rare.[2]

"Voices" are the most common type of Hallucination in Schizophrenia

Negative Symptoms

The term "negative symptoms" refers to reductions in normal emotional and behavioral states.These include the following:

- flat affect (immobile facial expression, monotonous voice),
- lack of pleasure in everyday life,
- diminished ability to initiate and sustain planned activity, and

- speaking infrequently, even when forced to interact.

People with schizophrenia often neglect basic hygiene and need help with everyday activities. Because it is not as obvious that negative symptoms are part of a psychiatric illness, people with schizophrenia are often perceived as lazy and unwilling to better their lives.

Cognitive Symptoms

Cognitive symptoms are subtle and are often detected only when neuropsychological tests are performed. They include the following:

- poor "executive functioning" (the ability to absorb and interpret information and make decisions based on that information),
- inability to sustain attention, and
- problems with "working memory" (the ability to keep recently learned information in mind and use it right away).

Cognitive impairments often interfere with the patient's ability to lead a normal life and earn a living. They can cause great emotional distress.

WHEN DOES IT START AND WHO GETS IT?

Psychotic symptoms (such as hallucinations and delusions) usually emerge in men in their late teens and early 20s and in women in their mid-20s to early 30s. They seldom occur after age 45 and only rarely before puberty, although cases of schizophrenia in children as young as 5 have been reported. In adolescents, the first signs can include a change of friends, a drop in grades, sleep problems, and irritability. Because many normal adolescents exhibit these behaviors as well, a diagnosis can be difficult to make at this stage. In young people who go on to develop the disease, this is called the "prodromal" period.

Research has shown that schizophrenia affects men and women equally and occurs at similar rates in all ethnic groups around the world.[3]

ARE PEOPLE WITH SCHIZOPHRENIA VIOLENT?

People with schizophrenia are not especially prone to violence and often prefer to be left alone. Studies show that if people have no record of criminal violence before they develop schizophrenia and are not substance abusers, they are unlikely to commit crimes after they become ill. Most violent crimes are not committed by people with schizophrenia, and most people with schizophrenia do not commit violent crimes. Substance abuse always increases violent behavior, regardless of the presence of schizophrenia (see sidebar). If someone with paranoid schizophrenia becomes violent, the violence is most often directed at family members and takes place at home.

WHAT ABOUT SUICIDE?

People with schizophrenia attempt suicide much more often than people in the general population. About 10 [4,5] percent (especially young adult males) succeed. It is hard to predict which people with schizophrenia are prone to suicide, so if someone talks about or tries to commit suicide, professional help should be sought right away.

> **People with Schizophrenia are not especially prone to violence and often prefer to be left alone.**

WHAT ABOUT SUBSTANCE ABUSE?

Some people who abuse drugs show symptoms similar to those of schizophrenia, and people with schizophrenia may be mistaken for people who are high on drugs. While most researchers do not believe that substance abuse causes schizophrenia, people who have schizophrenia abuse alcohol and/or drugs more often than the general population.

Substance abuse can reduce the effectiveness of treatment for schizophrenia. Stimulants (such as amphetamines or cocaine), PCP, and marijuana may make the symptoms of schizophrenia worse, and substance abuse also makes it more likely that patients will not follow their treatment plan.

Schizophrenia and Nicotine

The most common form of substance abuse in people with schizophrenia is an addiction to nicotine. People with schizo-phrenia are addicted to nicotine at three times the rate of the general population (75-90 percent vs. 25-30 percent).[6]

Research has revealed that the relationship between smoking and schizophrenia is complex. People with schizophrenia seem to be driven to smoke, and researchers are exploring whether there is a biological basis for this need. In addition to its known health hazards, several studies have found that smoking interferes with the action of antipsychotic drugs. People with schizophrenia who smoke may need higher doses of their medication.

Quitting smoking may be especially difficult for people with schizophrenia since nicotine withdrawal may cause their psychotic symptoms to temporarily get worse. Smoking cessation strategies that include nicotine replacement methods may be better tolerated. Doctors who treat people with schizophrenia should carefully monitor their patient's response to antipsychotic medication if the patient decides to either start or stop smoking.

WHAT CAUSES SCHIZOPHRENIA?

Like many other illnesses, schizophrenia is believed to result from a combination of environmental and genetic factors. All the tools of modern science are being used to search for the causes of this disorder.

Can Schizophrenia be Inherited?

Scientists have long known that schizophrenia runs in families. It occurs in 1 percent of the general population but is seen in 10 percent of people with a first-degree relative (a parent, brother, or sister) with the disorder. People who have second-degree relatives (aunts, uncles, grandparents, or cousins) with the disease also develop schizophrenia more often than the general population. The identical twin of a person with schizophrenia is most at risk, with a 40 to 65 percent chance of developing the disorder.[7]

Our genes are located on 23 pairs of chromosomes that are found in each cell. We inherit two copies of each gene, one from each parent. Several of these genes are thought to be asso-ciated with an increased risk of schizophrenia, but scientists believe that each gene has a very small effect and is not responsible for causing the disease by itself. It is still not possible to predict who will develop the disease by looking at genetic material.

Although there is a genetic risk for schizophrenia, it is not likely that genes alone are sufficient to cause the disorder. Interactions between genes and the environment are thought to be necessary for schizophrenia to develop. Many environmental factors have been suggested as risk factors, such as exposure to viruses or malnutrition in the womb, problems during birth, and psychosocial factors, like stressful environmental conditions.

> **People with Schizophrenia may be mistaken for people who are high on drugs.**

Do People with Schizophrenia Have Faulty Brain Chemistry?

It is likely that an imbalance in the complex, interrelated chemical reactions of the brain involving the neurotransmitters dopamine and glutamate (and possibly others) plays a role in schizophrenia. Neurotransmitters are substances that allow brain cells to communicate with one another. Basic knowledge about brain chemistry and its link to schizophrenia is expanding rapidly and is a promising area of research.

Do the Brains of People with Schizophrenia Look Different?

The brains of people with schizophrenia look a little different than the brains of healthy people, but the differences are small. Sometimes the fluid-filled cavities at the center of the brain, called ventricles, are larger in people with schizophrenia; overall gray matter volume is lower; and some areas of the brain have less or more metabolic activity.[3] Microscopic studies of brain tissue after death have also revealed small changes in the distribution or characteristics of brain cells in people with schizophrenia. It appears that many of these changes were prenatal because they are not accompanied by glial cells, which are always present when a brain injury occurs after birth.[3] One theory suggests that problems during brain development lead to faulty connections that lie dormant until puberty. The brain undergoes major changes during puberty, and these changes could trigger psychotic symptoms.

The only way to answer these questions is to conduct more research. Scientists in the United States and around the world are studying schizophrenia and trying to develop new ways to prevent and treat the disorder.

How Is Schizophrenia Treated?

Because the causes of schizophrenia are still unknown, current treatments focus on eliminating the symptoms of the disease.

Antipsychotic Medications

Antipsychotic medications have been available since the mid-1950s. They effectively alleviate the positive symptoms of schizophrenia. While these drugs have greatly improved the lives of many patients, they do not cure schizophrenia.

Everyone responds differently to antipsychotic medication. Sometimes several different drugs must be tried before the right one is found. People with schizophrenia should work in partnership with their doctors to find the medications that control their symptoms best with the fewest side effects.

The older antipsychotic medications include chlorpromazine (Thorazine®), haloperidol (Haldol®), perphenazine (Etrafon®, Trilafon®), and fluphenzine (Prolixin®). The older medications can cause extrapyramidal side effects, such as rigidity, persistent muscle spasms, tremors, and restlessness.

In the 1990s, new drugs, called atypical antipsychotics, were developed that rarely produced these side effects. The first of these new drugs was clozapine (Clozaril®). It treats psychotic symptoms effectively even in people who do not respond to other medications, but it can produce a serious problem called agranulocytosis, a loss of the white blood cells that fight infection. Therefore, patients who take clozapine must have their white blood cell counts monitored every week or two. The inconvenience and cost of both the blood tests and the med-ication itself has made treatment with clozapine difficult for many people, but it is the drug of choice for those whose symptoms do not respond to the other antipsychotic medica-tions, old or new.

Everyone responds differently to anti-sychotic medicaton.

Some of the drugs that were developed after clozapine was introduced—such as risperidone (Risperdal®), olanzapine (Zyprexa®), quetiapine (Seroquel®), sertindole (Serdolect®), and ziprasidone (Geodon ®)—are effective and rarely produce extrapyramidal symptoms and do not cause agranulocytosis; but they can cause weight gain and metabolic changes associated with an increased risk of diabetes and high cholesterol.[8]

People respond individually to antipsychotic medications, although agitation and hallucinations usually improve within days and delusions usually improve within a few weeks. Many people see substantial improvement in both types of symptoms by the sixth week of treatment. No one can tell beforehand exactly how a medication will affect a particular individual, and sometimes several medications must be tried before the right one is found.

When people first start to take atypical antipsychotics, they may become drowsy; experience dizziness when they change positions; have blurred vision; or develop a rapid heartbeat, menstrual problems, a sensitivity to the sun, or skin rashes. Many of these symptoms will go away after the first days of treatment, but people who are taking atypical antipsychotics should not drive until they adjust to their new medication.

If people with schizophrenia become depressed, it may be necessary to add an antidepressant to their drug regimen.

A large clinical trial funded by the National Institute of Mental Health (NIMH), known as CATIE (Clinical Antipsychotic Trials of Intervention Effectiveness), compared the effectiveness and side effects of five antipsychotic medications—both new and older antipsychotics—that are used to treat people with schizophrenia. For more information on CATIE, visit http://www.nimh.nih.gov/health information/catie.cfm.

Length of Treatment

Like diabetes or high blood pressure, schizophrenia is a chronic disorder that needs constant management. At the moment, it cannot be cured, but the rate of recurrence of psychotic episodes can be decreased significantly by staying on medication. Although responses vary from person to person, most people with schizophrenia need to take some type of medication for the rest of their lives as well as use other approaches, such as supportive therapy or rehabilitation.

Relapses occur most often when people with schizophrenia stop taking their antipsychotic medication because they feel better, or only take it occasionally because they forget or don't think taking it regularly is important. It is very important for people with schizophrenia to take their medication on a regular basis and for as long as their doctors recommend. If they do so, they will experience fewer psychotic symptoms.

No antipsychotic medication should be discontinued without talking to the doctor who prescribed it, and it should always be tapered off under a doctor's supervision rather than being stopped all at once.

There are a variety of reasons why people with schizophrenia do not adhere to treatment. If they don't believe they are ill, they may not think they need medication at all. If their thinking is too disorganized, they may not remember to take their medication every day. If they don't like the side effects of one medication, they may stop taking it without trying a different medication. Substance abuse can also interfere with treatment effectiveness. Doctors should ask patients how often they take their medication and be sensitive to a patient's request to change dosages or to try new medications to eliminate unwelcome side effects.

There are many strategies to help people with schizophrenia take their drugs regularly. Some medications are available in long-acting, injectable forms, which eliminate the need to take a pill every day. Medication calendars or pillboxes labeled with the days of the week can both help patients remember to take their medications and let caregivers know whether medication has been taken. Electronic timers on clocks or watches can be programmed to beep when people need to take their pills, and pairing medication with routine daily events, like meals, can help patients adhere to dosing schedules.

Medication Interactions

Antipsychotic medications can produce unpleasant or dangerous side effects when taken with certain other drugs.

For this reason, the doctor who prescribes the antipsychotics should be told about all medications (over-the-counter and prescription) and all vitamins, minerals, and herbal supplements the patient takes. Alcohol or other drug use should also be discussed.

At the moment, it can not be cured, but the rate of recurrence... can be decreased significantly...

Psychosocial Treatment

Numerous studies have found that psychosocial treatments can help patients who are already stabilized on antipsychotic medication deal with certain aspects of schizophrenia, such as difficulty with communication, motivation, self-care, work, and establishing and maintaining relationships with others. Learning and using coping mechanisms to address these problems allows people with schizophrenia to attend school, work, and socialize. Patients who receive regular psychosocial treatment also adhere better to their medication schedule and have fewer relapses and hospitalizations.A positive relationship with a therapist or a case manager gives the patient a reliable source of information, sympathy, encouragement, and hope, all of which are essential for for managing the disease. The therapist can help patients better understand and adjust to living with schizophrenia by educating them about the causes of the disorder, common symptoms or problems they may experience, and the importance of staying on medications.

Illness Management Skills
People with schizophrenia can take an active role in managing their own illness. Once they learn basic facts about schizophrenia and the principles of schizophrenia treatment, they can make informed decisions about their care. If they are taught how to monitor the early warning signs of relapse and make a plan to respond to these signs, they can learn to prevent relapses. Patients can also be taught more effective coping skills to deal with persistent symptoms.

> **Because the causes of Schizophrenia are still unknown, current treatments focus on eliminating the symptoms of the disease.**

Integrated Treatment for Co-occurring Substance Abuse
Substance abuse is the most common co-occurring disorder in people with schizophrenia, but ordinary substance abuse treatment programs usually do not address this population's special needs. Integrating schizophrenia treatment programs and drug treatment programs produces better outcomes.

Rehabilitation
Rehabilitation emphasizes social and vocational training to help people with schizophrenia function more effectively in their communities. Because people with schizophrenia frequently become ill during the critical career-forming years

of life (ages 18 to 35) and because the disease often interferes with normal cognitive functioning, most patients do not receive the training required for skilled work. Rehabilitation programs can include vocational counseling, job training, money management counseling, assistance in learning to use public transportation, and opportunities to practice social and workplace communication skills.

Family Education

Patients with schizophrenia are often dis-charged from the hospital into the care of their families, so it is important that family members know as much as possible about the disease to prevent relapses. Family members should be able to use different kinds of treatment adherence programs and have an arsenal of coping strategies and problem-solving skills to manage their ill relative effectively. Knowing where to find outpatient and family services that support people with schizophrenia and their caregivers is also valuable.

Cognitive Behavioral Therapy

Cognitive behavioral therapy is useful for patients with symptoms that persist even when they take medication. The cognitive therapist teaches people with schizophrenia how to test the reality of their thoughts and perceptions, how to "not listen" to their voices, and how to shake off the apathy that often immobilizes them. This treatment appears to be effective in reducing the severity of symptoms and decreasing the risk of relapse.

Self-Help Groups

Self-help groups for people with schizophrenia and their families are becoming increasingly common. Although professional therapists are not involved, the group members are a continuing source of mutual support and comfort for each other, which is also therapeutic. People in self-help groups know that others are facing the same problems they face and no longer feel isolated by their illness or the illness of their loved one.The networking that takes place in self-help groups can also generate social action. Families working together can advocate for research and more hospital and community treatment programs, and patients acting as a group may be able to draw public attention to the discriminations many people with mental illnesses still face in today's world.

Support groups and advocacy groups are excellent resources for people with many types of mental disorders.

WHAT IS THE ROLE OF THE PATIENT'S SUPPORT SYSTEM?

Support for those with mental disorders can come from families, professional residential or day program caregivers, shelter operators, friends or roommates, professional case managers, or others in their communities or places of worship who are concerned about their welfare. There are many situations in which people with schizophrenia will need help from other people.

Getting Treatment

People with schizophrenia often resist treatment, believing that their delusions or hallucinations are real and psychiatric help is not required. If a crisis occurs, family and friends may need to take action to keep their loved one safe.

The issue of civil rights enters into any attempt to provide treatment. Laws protecting patients from involuntary commitment have become very strict, and trying to get help for someone who is mentally ill can be frustrating. These laws vary from state to state, but, generally, when people are dangerous to themselves or others because of mental illness and refuse to seek treatment, family members or friends may have to call the police to transport them to the hospital. In the emergency room, a mental health professional will assess the patient and determine whether a voluntary or involuntary admission is needed.

A person with mental illness who does not want treatment may hide strange behavior or ideas from a professional; therefore, family members and friends should ask to speak pri-vately with the person conducting the patient's examination and explain what has been happening at home. The professional will then be able to question the patient and hear the patient's distorted thinking for themselves. Professionals must personally witness bizarre behavior and hear delusional thoughts before they can legally recommend commitment, and family and friends can give them the information they need to do so.

> **Family and friends can also help patients set realistic goals and regain their ability to function in the world.**

Caregiving

Ensuring that people with schizophrenia continue to get treatment and take their medication after they leave the hospital is also important. If patients stop taking their medication or stop going for follow-up appointments, their psychotic symptoms will return. If these symptoms become severe, they may become unable to care for their own basic needs for food, clothing, and shelter; they may neglect personal hygiene; and they may end up on the street or in jail, where they rarely receive the kind of help they need.

Family and friends can also help patients set realistic goals and regain their ability to function in the world. Each step toward these goals should be small enough to be attainable, and the patient should pursue them in an atmosphere of support. People with a mental illness who are pressured and criticized usually regress and their symptoms worsen. Telling them what they are doing right is the best way to help them move forward.

How should you respond when someone with schizophrenia makes statements that are strange or clearly false? Because these bizarre beliefs or hallucinations are real to the patient, it will not be useful to say they are wrong or imaginary. Going along with the delusions will not be helpful, either. It is best to calmly say that you see things differently than the patient does but that you acknowledge that everyone has the right to see things in his or her own way. Being respectful, supportive, and kind without tolerating dangerous or inappropriate behavior is the most helpful way to approach people with this disorder.

WHAT IS THE OUTLOOK FOR THE FUTURE?

The outlook for people with schizophrenia has improved over the last 30 years or so. Although there still is no cure, effective treatments have been developed, and many people with schizophrenia improve enough to lead independent, satisfying lives.

This is an exciting time for schizophrenia research. The explosion of knowledge in genetics, neuroscience, and behavioral research will enable a better understanding of the causes of the disorder, how to prevent it, and how to develop better treatments to allow those with schizophrenia to achieve their full potential.

This is an exciting time for Schizophrenia Research.

HOW CAN A PERSON PARTICIPATE
IN SCHIZOPHRENIA RESEARCH?

Scientists worldwide are studying schizophrenia so they will be able to develop new ways to prevent and treat the disorder. The only way it can be understood is for researchers to study the illness as it presents itself in those who suffer from it. There are many different kinds of studies. Some studies require that medication be changed; others, like genetic studies, require no change at all in medications.

To receive online information about federally and privately supported schizophrenia research, visit http://clinicaltrials.gov. This site describes an extensive list of studies being conducted across the United States. The information provided should be used in conjunction with advice from a health care professional.

NIMH conducts a Schizophrenia Research Program, which is located at the National Institute of Mental Health in Bethesda, Maryland. Travel assistance and study compensation are available for some studies. A list of outpatient and inpatient studies conducted at NIMH can be found at http://patientinfo.nimh.nih.gov. In addition, NIMH staff members can speak with you and help you determine whether their current studies are suitable for you or your family member. Simply call the toll free line at **1-888-674-6464**. You can also indicate your interest in research participation by sending an email to Schizophrenia@intra.nimh.nih.gov. All calls remain confidential.

Addendum to Schizophrenia January 2007

Aripiprazole (Abilify) is another atypical antipsychotic medication used to treat the symptoms of schizophrenia and manic or mixed (manic and depressive) episodes of bipolar I disorder. Aripiprazole is in tablet and liquid form. An injectable form is used in the treatment of symptoms of agitation in schizophrenia and manic or mixed episodes of bipolar I disorder.

REFERENCES

[1] Regier, DA; Narrow, WE; Rae, DS; Manderscheid, RW; Locke, BZ & Goodwin, FK. (1993). The de facto US mental and addictive disorders service system. Epidemiologic catchment area prospective 1-year prevalence rates of disorders and services. *Arch Gen Psychiatry*. Feb; *50(2)*:85-94.

[2] Catatonic Schizophrenia. (1992). *The ICD-10 Classification of Mental and Behavioural Disorders: Clinical descriptions and diagnostic guidelines*. Geneva, Switzerland: World Health Organization.

[3]   Mueser, KT & McGurk, SR. (2004). Schizophrenia. *Lancet.* Jun 19;
       363(9426):2063-72.

[4]   Meltzer, HY; Alphs, L; Green, AI; Altamura, AC; Anand, R; Bertoldi, A;
       Bourgeois, M; Chouinard, G; Islam, MZ; Kane, J; Krishnan, R;
       Lindenmayer, JP; Potkin, S & International Suicide Prevention Trial Study
       Group. (2003). Clozapine treatment for suicidality in schizophrenia:
       International Suicide Prevention Trial (InterSePT). *Arch Gen Psychiatry.*
       Jan; *60(1)*:82-91.

[5]   Meltzer, HY & Baldessarini, RJ. (2003). Reducing the risk for suicide in
       schizophrenia and affective disorders. *J Clin Psychiatry.* Sep; *64(9)*:1122-9.

[6]   Jones, RT & Benowitz, NL. (2002). Therapeutics for Nicotine Addiction. In
       Davis KL, Charney D, Coyle JT & Nemeroff C (Eds.), *Neuropsycho
       pharmacology: The Fifth Generation of Progress* (pp1533-1544). Nashville,
       TN:American College of Neuropsychopharmacology.

[7]   Cardno, AG & Gottesman, II. (2000). Twin studies of schizo-phrenia: from
       bow-and-arrow concordances to star wars Mx and functional genomics. *Am
       J Med Genet. Spring; 97(1)*:12-7.

[8]   Lieberman, JA; Stroup, TS; McEvoy, JP; Swartz, MS; Rosenheck, RA;
       Perkins, DO; Keefe, RS; Davis, SM; Davis, CE; Lebowitz, BD; Severe, J &
       Hsiao, JK. (2005). Clinical Antipsychotic Trials of Intervention
       Effectiveness (CATIE). Effectiveness of antipsychotic drugs in patients
       with chronic schizophrenia. *N Engl J Med.* Sep 22; *353(12)*:1209-23.

FOR MORE INFORMATION ON SCHIZOPHRENIA

The National Library of Medicine, a service of the U.S. Library of Medicine
and the National Institutes of Health, provides updated information on many
health topics, including schizophrenia. It also lists mental health organizations that
provide useful information. If you have Internet access, search for schizophrenia
at http://medlineplus.gov.

En Espanol http://medlineplus.gov/spanish/

Information from NIMH is available in multiple formats.You can browse
online, download documents in PDF, and order paper brochures through the mail.
If you would like to have NIMH publications, you can order them online at
www.nimh.nih.gov. If you do not have Internet access and wish to have
information that supplements this publication, please contact the NIMH
Information Center at the numbers listed below.

FOR FURTHER INFORMATION

National Institute of Mental Health
Public Inquiries & Dissemination Branch
6001 Executive Boulevard
Room 8184, MSC 9663
Bethesda, MD 20892-9663
Phone: 301-443-5413 or
1-866-615-NIMH (6464) toll-free
TTY: 301-443-8431
TTY: 866-415-8051
FAX: 301-443-4279
E-mail: nimhinfo@nih.gov
Web site: http://www.nimh.nih.gov.

This publication is in the public domain and may be reproduced or copied without permission from the National Institute of Mental Health (NIMH). NIMH encourages you to reproduce this publication and use it in your efforts to improve public health. Citation of the NIMH as a source is appreciated. However, using government materials inappropriately can raise legal or ethical concerns, so we ask you to use these guidelines:

- NIMH does not endorse or recommend any commercial products, processes, or services and this publication may not be used for advertising or endorsement purposes.
- NIMH does not provide specific medical advice or treatment recommendations or referrals; these materials may not be used in a manner that has the appearance of such information.
- NIMH requests that Non-Federal organizations not alter this publication in a way that will jeopardize the integrity and "brand" when using the publication.
- Addition of Non-Federal Government logos and website links may not have the appearance of NIMH endorsement of any specific commercial products or services or medical treatments or services.

If you have questions regarding these guidelines and use of NIMH publications please contact the NIMH Information Center at 1-866-615-6464 or email at nimhinfo@nih.gov.

CHAPTER SOURCES

The following chapters have been previously published

Chapter 1 – This is an edited, reformatted and augmented version of a National Institute of Mental Health Report, with Addendum "Bipolar Disorder" Dated January 2007.

Chapter 2 – This is an edited, reformatted and augmented version adapted by Melissa Spearing, Office of Communications and Public Liaison, National Institute of Mental Health from "Bipolar Disorder," NIH Publication Number 01-3679. Dated, 2002.

Chapter 3 – This is an edited, reformatted and augmented version a National Institute on Drug Abuse, Research Report Series, "Comorbidity: Addiction and Other Mental Illnesses. NIH Publication Number 08-5771, Dated December 2008.

Chapter 4 – This is an edited, reformatted and augmented version of a National Institute of Mental Health Report, with Addendum Schizophrenia, Dated January 2007.

INDEX

C

N

O